TAKING THE SHOT

THE DAVIDSON BASKETBALL MOMENT

MICHAEL KRUSE

ISBN 978-1-884532-98-6

Book Design by Scott Stortz

Cover photo: © Thad Allender/LJWorld.com/KUSports.com
All other photos: © 2008 Tim Cowie
All photographs are reprinted with permission of the photographers.

Stories included from *Charlotte* magazine and DavidsonCats.com
were reprinted with permission.

Printed in USA

Published by
Butler Books
P.O. Box 7311
Louisville, KY 40207
(502) 897-9393
Fax (502) 897-9797

www.butlerbooks.com

To my parents,
Jens Kruse and Susan Kunk,
who keep opening doors

Table of Contents

Prologue	vii
Narrative: Taking the Shot	1
Epilogue	63
Acknowledgments	65
Interviews	67
Photos	73-88
Additional Stories about Davidson Basketball	89
Sources and Notes	133

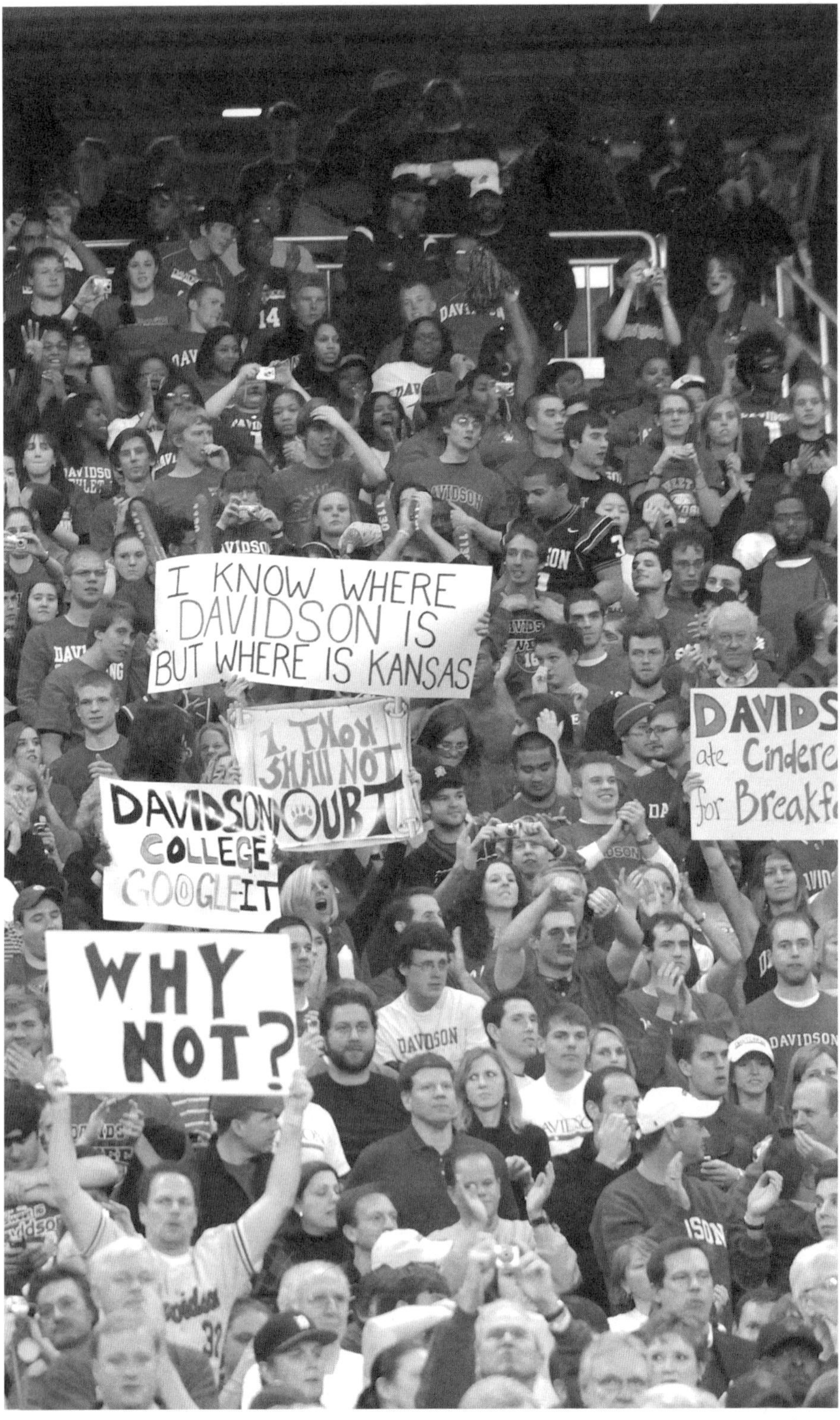
I KNOW WHERE DAVIDSON IS BUT WHERE IS KANSAS
DAVIDSON COLLEGE GOOGLE IT
WHY NOT?
DAVIDS
ate Cindere
for Breakf

PROLOGUE

In March 2008, the basketball team from Davidson College in Davidson, North Carolina, won a game in the NCAA tournament, then another, then another after that – Gonzaga, Georgetown, Wisconsin – and that led to a game against perennial national power Kansas for the right to go to the Final Four. Davidson is a small school, with an enrollment of about 1,700 students, and in a small town, with a population of not even 10,000 people, and so this accomplishment was tagged by many with a term that often is used in sports to describe any eye-catching combination of an unknown doing the unexpected.

"Cinderella Davidson."

"Cinderella Dances On."

"Davidson Extends Cinderella Run."

Those were the headlines. But this was not that. Or at least it wasn't only that.

There was a coach in Bob McKillop who talked in news conferences about discipline and love and balance. There was a sophomore superstar in Stephen Curry who wrote scripture on his sneakers and looked like a kid and shot like a pro. There was a steady senior leader in Jason Richards who had barely even played in his first two years on the team. There were selfless players from Maine and Cincinnati and Staten Island and France and Nigeria and Quebec. And they were backed by the kind of town and campus and community for which people seemed to be nostalgic. America, one sports columnist wrote, fell "stone-cold in love."

Davidson College was the No. 1 search on Google after the team's win over Georgetown. Davidson was mentioned 9,000 times in the print media in March. Davidson.edu got 1.2 million hits. The Kansas game was watched by a record crowd of 57,000 in Ford Field in Detroit and on national TV on CBS by 13.6 million people. Almost one in five televisions in the country that were turned on were turned to the game.

But the interest went beyond even the numerical. Sports columnists called the team "young America at its finest" and "a little slice of what's right." One even said "a Davidson victory is what's best for the world."

People saw something they wanted to see.

What was it?

The Kansas game was close. It came down to the last minute. It came down to the last moment of the last minute.

"Cinderella" in sports parlance suggests a sequence of events touched by luck. The idea is that it's fun but also fluky, even fleeting – a visible, ephemeral blip of what some might call magic or fate.

But the moment at the end of Davidson's game against Kansas was not a happy accident. It was powerful because it was created by many people doing many things for many years. And in that moment, and throughout Davidson's games in March, most of the people who were doing the Google searches and following on CBS and standing and watching the game in Detroit were responding in an intangible, unconscious way to the idea that there was something more at work here. This was not just a simple Cinderella tale. People might not have known the specifics of the story, but they knew what they felt: Maybe there was a secret somewhere in there. Maybe there was a lesson.

TAKING THE SHOT

THE DAVIDSON BASKETBALL MOMENT

KANSAS HAD HAD THE BALL AND THE LEAD. The score was 59-57. A guard had dribbled to his right, then to his left, and had taken an off-balance three-pointer that bounced off the rim and out of bounds. Now the crowd was louder than even before.

"Davidson!" the CBS play-by-play man yelled.

The Ford Field clocks showed 16.8 seconds left.

"With life!"

The camera shifted to the Davidson sideline and zeroed in on the face of the coach.

Bob McKillop, silver-white hair, sharp blue eyes, trim dark suit, walked slowly up the sideline in front of his team's bench.

He was 57 years old and by this point he had won more games than any coach in Davidson history and more games than any coach in Southern Conference history. He had been the league's coach of the year a record seven times. All 62 of his senior players had graduated, math majors, economics majors, political science majors. But McKillop still was relatively unknown by casual fans of the sport. He had before this tournament never beaten a team ranked in the Top 25 poll or won a game in the NCAAs. Within his profession, though, he was respected as a meticulous, almost professorial tactician, intense and ultra-competitive and yet finger-snap quick to get wet-eyed when talking about his family, or his team, or both.

Don't guard yourself, he tells his players. Don't let missteps in the past lead to more in the future.

Two words: Next play.

Now, here on the sideline, he looked out at his players on the court. He nodded his head once, then twice, and he tried to "read" them – especially Stephen Curry and Jason Richards, his two best guards. He had coached Jason for four years and Stephen for two, and now he looked for something subtle, some bit of body language, a facial expression, anything that would tell him: *Coach, we got it.*

What he saw was: *Coach, give us some direction.*

So he called a timeout. His last of the game.

His career at Davidson had started 19 years before, in old Johnston Gym, in a small upstairs office with a window unit air conditioner and a red shag carpet. Davidson was decades past its basketball prime.

In 1960, the folksy, strong-willed Lefty Driesell came to coach at Davidson. Back then Davidson had mandated attendance at church services and an enrollment of less than 1,000 men. The basketball team had had four winning seasons since World War II and had won only five games the year before Driesell arrived. But the difference with Driesell was immediate: His first team in its first game beat Atlantic Coast Conference power Wake Forest. He started recruiting players who went on to become

All-Americans. By the time he left, in 1969, to coach at the University of Maryland, he had taken Davidson to 176 wins, four top-10 finishes in the Associated Press poll and consecutive appearances in the NCAA regional finals.

Driesell had been a high school coach in Virginia before coming to Davidson. McKillop was the same way. He had been a high school coach in New York at Trinity High in Hicksville and at Long Island Lutheran in Brookville. He had gone to eight state final fours in 13 years, had coached five high school All-Americans and had been the *New York Daily News* coach of the year four times.

When he arrived in Davidson, he put in his office a copy of the *Sports Illustrated* from 1964 in which Davidson was ranked No. 1 in the country, and also the one from 1968 when Davidson star forward Mike Maloy was on the cover.

He said he was going to do that again.

But Driesell had started at Davidson before all-black Texas Western beat all-white Kentucky for the national championship in 1966 to alter the racial makeup of the college game. He had started before all-sports, all-the-time ESPN started in 1979 to make exposure spike, and before CBS agreed in 1999 to pay the NCAA $6 billion over 11 years for the exclusive rights to televise the "March Madness" tournament that has become a three-week, coast-to-coast cultural phenomenon.

During the years between Driesell and McKillop, Davidson had five different basketball coaches, and three more took the job and left without ever coaching a game. It was a decade and a half of not only too many losses but also a hopelessness that came with the realization that the nationally competitive basketball program of the '60s had come, and had gone, and maybe for good. Davidson's athletic program as a whole was unstable and uncompetitive. Many professors saw it as a waste of money and were urging the school to drop from Division I to Division III.

McKillop actually was uneasy enough to turn down the Davidson job in early May 1989 before he accepted a second offer three weeks later. He wasn't a stranger to Davidson: He had been a guard on the team at East Carolina that lost to Davidson in the 1969 Southern Conference championship game in Charlotte. He was an assistant coach at Davidson 10 years after that and liked to tell the guys on the team that year that he was a "mustard sandwich sort of guy."

Ten years after that he was the head coach.

And cocky.

Sterling Freeman was on the team that first year. He was at home in Arkansas over the summer and got a call from the new coach.

"Are you a dreamer?" McKillop asked him.

"You need to understand," the new coach told him. "I'm expecting big things."

But big things did not happen.

McKillop's first year ended with a record of four wins and 24 losses.

His second year wasn't much better: 10 wins and 19 losses.

His third year: 11 wins and 17 losses.

But in the first team meeting that fall of 1989, the players sat on red wooden stools in the small locker room in old Johnston Gym, and McKillop told them he was on a mission.

He was going places.

He invited them to join him.

Then he made them do sprints on the track and five-mile runs around campus in the semi-dark of hazy early mornings. Hurricane Hugo came through the Carolinas in September and raked the Charlotte area and knocked a big tree down across the Davidson track.

"Run around it," he told them.

"There were times," one former player once said, "when we thought he was going to kill us."

"I was in survival mode," said another.

After a lopsided loss to Miami of Ohio McKillop called them fat and slow in the locker room and then didn't turn the heat on in the bus on the way to the airport.

At one point he tied an electrical socket to his torso and told his players to plug into him if they needed extra energy.

Late in the season, A.J. Morgan, a guard, had a roommate whose father died. He went to the funeral and missed a game because of it. McKillop called him into his office. He was not happy.

"I think he felt like it was a violation of the team," Morgan would say later. "He was sort of letting me know that there was only one mission in his life at that time."

But that first year wasn't the low point, and it wasn't the breaking point.

That came at the end of the third year.

In Anderson, South Carolina, Davidson lost in the conference tournament quarterfinals. This was the first week of March 1992. The only reason fans weren't calling for McKillop to be fired was that there weren't that many fans. The Davidson booster club had rented a room at the Anderson Holiday Inn for post-game cold cuts and bottles of Bud. Maybe 15 people were there. McKillop gave a short talk. It felt like a wake. It was raining hard outside, and McKillop left his wife and his three young children to go watch a prospect at a local junior college. He drove away from the hotel straining to see through the rain.

McKillop had come from high school coaching to college coaching and thought he could get respect from his players by talking tough. His players at Davidson back then thought he knew enough about basketball strategy, and they saw him working long hours, and they wanted to believe in him.

But they didn't.

McKillop talked about where he was going. He talked less about where they actually were.

After the game in Anderson, McKillop questioned his decision to leave New York and doubted his ability ever to win at Davidson, or in college at all. He had come to Davidson intent on winning – fast – so he could move to a better, more lucrative, more prestigious job. It was all about him, and what he was going to do, and how he was going to do it. What *he* was doing, though, was not working.

That electrical socket gimmick?

Energy, he realized, isn't a one-way deal. Everyone has energy. The point is to share it.

"I came to the conclusion," he would say years later, "that I had done a disservice to my players by thinking only what winning would do for me rather than giving them an experience they could cherish for the rest of their lives. … After that miserable night in Anderson, I decided to tell the guys that winning and losing doesn't matter. But if we care about each other, and show we care about each other, winning will take care of itself."

He decided then on a three-word code for the basketball program at

Davidson, borrowing the words from Lou Holtz, then the football coach at Notre Dame.

Trust. Commitment. Care.

Those three words started off as letters printed on T-shirts and painted on a sign on the locker room wall. Over the years, slowly, they came to mean more than that.

Now, in Detroit, during the timeout, he met with his four assistant coaches, standing off to the side of his players.

McKillop asked them all a question.

"What do you think?"

The stands at Ford Field had turned into the biggest, best-attended Davidson reunion ever. The people in the crowd in the sections behind the team's bench were dressed mostly in red and ranged from graduates from the 1930s to incoming freshmen, practically a century of the life of the college. Alums had cancelled plans, rented cars and booked plane tickets and hotel rooms with disregard for credit card bills and prior plans. Almost all the college's trustees had contributed their own money so that nearly a third of the student body could be bused to Detroit for the weekend. The final tally was 12 buses, 86 hotel rooms, almost 600 students, and a tab of $190,000. The Dearborn Doubletree had become a Davidson dorm. Students sat at tables in the lobby and spread out around the floor and opened their laptops to work on term papers and tests.

But inside Ford Field, against Wisconsin two days before, and then against Kansas, too, they held signs high above their heads.

WHY NOT?

THOU SHALL NOT DOUBT

Now they were chanting.

"We be-lieve!"

"We be-lieve!"

"We be-lieve!"

Many of them were wearing new red shirts that had on the front one word written in white block font. WITNESS. The shirts had been handed out by the school for the Wisconsin game two days before. They seemed appropriate that night because LeBron James, the NBA star who uses "witness" as one of his Nike-pitched buzzwords, was in a seat a few rows behind the Davidson bench. He was there, he told reporters, "to watch the kid." Stephen. The WITNESS shirts were cool, but not quite right, some of the students thought. They weren't just *watching* this. They felt like they were a *part* of it. They knew all the guys down there in the huddle. They took cognitive psychology with them. They got calculus help from them. They played pickup basketball on the outdoor courts with them. They ate the same food at the same cafeteria at Vail Commons. They knew from parties on fraternity row at Patterson Court who the team's best dancer was and who had no rhythm at all.

When the players looked up into the stands, they sometimes said, they didn't see fans. They saw friends. What they shared, the students off the court and the students on it, was a place: a college with white-pillar buildings and red-brick walkways known for graduating future doctors, lawyers and preachers, not basketball stars; a town with one bar, a barbershop, an independent bookstore and a greasy spoon called the Soda Shop on a Main Street that looked like a painting by Norman

Rockwell; and a campus where life was dictated by Davidson's Honor Code, which meant unsupervised final exams, communal yellow bikes anyone could use, forgotten watches left at the front desk at the rec center and lost dollar bills thumb-tacked to bulletin boards.

Now everybody, everywhere, they thought, was learning a little about their place.

At a game earlier in the season a fan had held up a sign that said this:

YOU MAKE US PROUD

"There they were – facing the world that couldn't help staring back," sophomore English major Claire Asbury wrote in her journal in March.

"They come from us, as we come from them. That's what Davidson is, I think; we create each other, appreciate each other, take joy in each other. And it's not just students; it's those who used to be students, teachers, elders, children, staff, players, coaches …

"Life joining with life," she wrote.

In Detroit, during the games, the Davidson students in the stands had felt the faces and the eyes of the rest of the crowd turn toward them during timeouts.

At first it seemed strange, but then they started to wonder.

What were they looking at?

Maybe, some of them thought, the people at Ford Field wanted to be a part of *something* the way the kids from Davidson felt a part of this.

Down on the court McKillop finished talking to his assistants and walked over to his players.

"What do you guys want to do?" he asked.

"What do you think about Flat?"

Davidson calls the play Flat because the first important action is what is known as a flat ball screen. A post player comes from under the basket to the top of the key and sets a pick with his back parallel to the baseline. "Flat." A teammate dribbles toward the screen and goes either right or left. The aim is to free the man with the ball by screening his defender. That's if the play works.

Davidson doesn't use the play every year. Flat is best with a skilled, savvy dribbler and shooter, and Davidson doesn't always have a player like that. When Davidson does use it, though, it's used most often in late-clock or late-game situations.

In 2008 it was run for pretty much just one guy.

McKillop looked at Stephen now.

The Kansas defenders who had been teaming up to guard Stephen were tall, fast and lanky-armed. They had held him nearly scoreless in the last nine minutes of the game. He had 25 points but had made only four of the 16 three-pointers he had taken.

Stephen was exhausted.

But the coach couldn't risk not having the ball in the hands of his best player on this game's final play. The easiest way to avoid that was to put it there right away.

McKillop looked at Stephen.

He asked again.

"What do you think about Flat?"

The boy-faced 20-year-old son of former NBA shooting guard Dell Curry had become the star of the tournament. His regular season had been one of the best in the country: almost 26 points per game, Southern Conference player of the year, Associated Press All-American. Stephen already was one of the most important players in the history of Davidson basketball – that had taken two years – and 10 days of the tournament had made him a national name. Most people even learned how to pronounce it: Steff-in.

He looks like the kid next door, he looks like the kid who cut the grass, he looks like the water boy. That's what people were saying. He looks like he's 11, he looks like he's 12, he looks like he's just been Bar Mitzvahed.

He didn't *look* like he should be able to do what he was doing.

He scored 40 points against Gonzaga and the Gonzaga coach told reporters his players probably had guarded him as well as they could have. He scored 30 against Georgetown and the Georgetown coach said his defenders had been "all over him." He scored 33 against Wisconsin in a Davidson rout that felt almost anticlimactic.

Seldom is the best player in the tournament also the best story. But Stephen was both. Part of the appeal was his "soundbite story" that worked so well on CBS: *Everybody said he was too small.*

People could relate.

Stephen had picked Davidson over schools like Winthrop and Virginia Commonwealth. The big basketball programs at Atlantic Coast Conference schools didn't want him. The only ACC school that recruited him even a bit was Virginia Tech, and that was his parents' alma mater. Even there the coaches wanted him to walk on as a freshman and wait for a scholarship.

There was reason for that: As a freshman at Charlotte Christian

School Stephen was 5-foot-6 and so thin the coaches put him on the junior varsity team. He made the varsity as a sophomore but he was still only 5-foot-8. As a junior he was 5-foot-11. As a senior he was 6-foot-1. But now in the huddle he was 6-foot-2. He hadn't stopped growing.

Back in high school, though, a typical scouting evaluation started like this: "Way overmatched from a physical standpoint."

But McKillop and the Davidson assistant coaches look at prospects differently than many other college programs. They have to. Davidson is not in one of the country's most powerful leagues and so it isn't going to get the sure-thing recruits. Davidson's admissions office lets in only one in four students who apply. No exceptions. Not even for basketball players. Fewer than 1,700 students, classes with 15 students – there's no place to hide someone who can't do the rigorous academic work.

Davidson once recruited a short, slow-footed kid from New York City by watching him play a volleyball game in Brooklyn and shoot around in his gym in Manhattan. Peter Anderer became the MVP of the Southern Conference tournament in 2002.

Davidson once recruited a skinny-armed, pasty-faced point guard from Ireland who in his first game couldn't get the ball over half-court. In his senior season Michael Bree hit a key three-pointer and made a critical pass in the final minute that helped Davidson beat North Carolina in Chapel Hill.

Davidson once recruited a nerdy, thin tall boy from a boarding school in northern England, where he practiced basketball only one hour a week. Before too long Chris Pearson was blocking shots against Duke.

McKillop and his assistants look for prospects from around the country and around the world who can run, jump, shoot and pass. But those basics are only the beginning of the evaluation.

What does a prospect do when his coach takes him out of the game? Does he walk over to the bench or does he run? How does he sit? Does he mope? Does he high-five his teammates?

Does he take big shots? Does he want to?

There's a loose ball on the floor. Does he dive head-first? Or is he scared of getting hurt?

Is he an eye-roller?

Is he a shoulder-shrugger?

How does he talk to his mother?

Does he know the janitor with the keys to the gym?

With Stephen, what Davidson coaches saw when they started scouting him were shots going in, and sharp passes, and a baggy jersey hanging off his slender shoulders.

But McKillop also watched him warm up in layup lines. He wasn't cool, and the coach liked that. Cool, he believes, is someone who wants people to watch. Cool is a sense of entitlement. Stephen wasn't cool.

Something else all the coaches noticed over time was that Stephen's face almost never changed. He made a three-pointer and his face didn't change. He missed a three-pointer and his face didn't change. He made a great pass, he made an awful pass, he turned the ball over, a teammate turned the ball over – his face didn't change.

"I saw him make mistakes," McKillop would say later, "and not pout about it."

And he saw constant, relentless improvement.

By his senior year, Stephen led Charlotte Christian to two wins over favored teams from big public schools from South Carolina and

Georgia in a tournament before Christmas, then another championship in a tournament after Christmas. Dave Telep, a scout for Scout.com, had seen Stephen play in all three of his high school varsity seasons, and in his report for college coaches, Telep wrote, in capital letters, "HUGE upside."

Telep based his evolving opinion not only on what he saw from Stephen but also on what he saw from Stephen's parents. He watched Dell Curry hang signs in the gym. He watched Sonya Curry keep the scorebook at her son's games. He saw a family.

In early September of Stephen's senior year of high school, on the first day college coaches were allowed to go on the road recruiting, three Davidson coaches – the most allowed by NCAA rules – went to Charlotte Christian to visit Stephen. A little more than a week later, when they were visiting him at his house in Charlotte, he told the coaches he had made up his mind: He wanted to go to Davidson. He surprised everybody but himself. He hadn't even told his parents.

McKillop bear-hugged Stephen.

"Coach," Stephen's mother told McKillop. "We'll get him fattened up for you."

McKillop smiled.

"We'll take him," he told her, "just the way he is."

That spring, in 2006, Davidson graduated seven seniors who had scored more than 75 percent of the points for a team that had gone to the NCAA tournament. Davidson fans were worried. But at the year-end banquet, McKillop gave a speech, and at the end, in front of the hundreds of fans that night, he said he had one word for the coming year.

"Surprise!"

People thought he was nuts.

That summer, though, word started to trickle out of the Charlotte pro-am league. Dell Curry's boy could play.

That September, Danny Smith, a big Davidson fan and a close friend to McKillop, was out in his boat on nearby Lake Norman with the coach.

"Stephen," McKillop told him, "has the ability to be one of the best basketball players ever to put on a Davidson jersey."

Smith was stunned.

"Really?"

McKillop never talked like this.

"Really," McKillop said.

Telep sent an e-mail that fall to a contact of his in the front office of an NBA team. "I'm going to give you a name," he wrote, "that someday I think is going to come into prominence."

By the time he showed up at Davidson for the fall of his freshman year, Stephen was bigger, stronger, faster, taller. He was a better shooter. He was a better passer. He was a better dribbler. All of that, though, was not what struck the Davidson coaches the most.

Pre-season workouts in the fall are hard. They are especially hard for freshmen. College basketball is far faster and more intricate than high school play. Coaches have to stop after every drill and tell players what they're doing right, what they're doing wrong, and what they should do instead. Those adjustments take time.

Except with Stephen.

He was able to take the information given to him and correct his mistakes almost immediately. He had 13 turnovers in his first college game. He had 32 points in his second, against Michigan, in Ann Arbor. McKillop had been coaching three and a half decades, and had never seen a player like him. It was as if Stephen listened to what he was told, painted a picture of the movements in his head, and then channeled those movements onto the court, at full speed, the very next play.

Now, in the huddle in Detroit, Stephen paused to think.

McKillop watched him do that.

Across from Stephen in the huddle was Jason Richards.

The point guard from the Chicago suburb of Barrington, Illinois, had played very little in his freshman and sophomore seasons at Davidson. In his junior year, though, he had the second-most assists in the country; as a senior, nobody had more. Against Wisconsin, two days before, he had passed for 13 assists and no turnovers – unheard of – to help Davidson get to this game against Kansas. One of the Wisconsin players had said Jason was one of the best point guards he had ever played against.

Lots of people called him underrated. He had gotten used to backhanded compliments like "deceptively quick." All Jason did was take the ball where he wanted to take it, and where he needed to take it, against just about everybody, just about always. He didn't see his teammates *when* they were open. He saw them when they were *getting* open. Pause Davidson game tape, and there is the ball, in the air, between

Jason's hand and a spot on the floor where Stephen is *about* to be.

Jason didn't run the team's plays.

He ran the team.

Early on in his Davidson career, though, people weren't so sure. He wasn't recruited by a lot of big-name basketball schools. He picked Davidson over Colgate and Yale. The fall of his first year he got a leg cramp in the college's silly annual freshman class cake race and wasn't even able to finish. He got so winded in his first individual workout that McKillop started calling him "Crisco."

McKillop is known for how hard he is on point guards in practice. He's especially hard on freshmen, and even harder on point guards who are freshmen, and hardest on those who have the greatest potential. He was relentless with Jason. The student managers from those years still talk about it.

Jason played eight minutes a game as a backup in his first year at Davidson.

As a sophomore he showed occasional promise.

That year, in a close game in November against St. Joseph's, he had to play. The starting point guard fouled out in the last minute. Earlier in the game Jason had gone back to the locker room because he had eaten for breakfast some bad bacon and eggs. But in the last minute of the game, plus the five-minute overtime, he scored 10 points to finish with a career-high 13 to lead Davidson to a win.

That year in the NCAA tournament, though, he played poorly. In a close loss he was scared by the bigness of the moment.

After the game, back at the team's hotel, Jason was with his father in the lobby, and McKillop went over to him.

"Twelve o'clock rule," the coach said.

Jason had until midnight to think about the game and his performance. Then it was over.

When Jason was a freshman in high school in Barrington, Illinois, the basketball coach had called his father to ask him if he could put Jason on the varsity team. Jason was 5-foot-6 and 120 pounds, pre-pubescent, but he was so skilled, the coach thought, that he could play varsity. The worry was whether Jason was ready for that. So the coach went to the father.

Tom Richards had put his son in basketball camps all over western Pennsylvania. That's where the family lived before Illinois. He started an all-dribbling club called the Little Panthers for kids in the third, fourth, fifth and sixth grades, and he put Jason in it when he was in the first grade. He drove Jason into Pittsburgh and put him in the league for sixth-graders when he was a third-grader. And he had him play his sister on the asphalt court behind their house. Lindsay Richards was two years older and was a high school McDonald's All-American. But they had grown up playing ferocious one-on-one games. Defense called fouls. There were not a lot of fouls called. Jason and Lindsay went at each other until Tom Richards said stop.

Jason, the father told the coach, had always played against opponents who were older, bigger and stronger. It was how he had learned to take advantage of what he could do and hide what he could not.

Jason not only played varsity his freshman year at Barrington. He started.

The crowds at away games that season were merciless with their chants.

In his first game, at Mundelein High School in Mundelein, Illinois, he was introduced and he ran out onto the court. He was still a boy, and Lindsay almost couldn't watch. She sat in the stands hoping her little brother wouldn't get hurt.

The crowd was all over him.

"Wherrre's your momm-mmmmy?"

Every time he touched the ball.

"Wherrre's your momm-mmmmy?"

It didn't stop.

"Wherrre's your momm-mmmmy?"

In the second half his mother stood up in the stands.

"I'm right here!" Mary Beth Richards yelled, jabbing both forefingers at herself. "I'm right here!"

The first time any coach from Davidson saw Jason play was about a year and a half after that. It was at a club tournament in Orlando the summer after his sophomore year of high school and one of Jason's games went into six overtimes. Davidson assistant Jim Fox was there.

Summer club-team basketball is about showcasing individual skills. It's not about who wins tournaments; it's me, not we. But Fox watched Jason play in this game, in this game in the summer that went *six* overtimes, and he could see that Jason very badly wanted to win.

Davidson's coaches started recruiting him.

The next summer he played with a different club team. The coach of the team thought Jason looked like a shortstop, not a point guard. He was small but smart. He understood what he could do, but also, and maybe more importantly, what he could not. He had a fast first step and he used it to get by a defender, even just a little, and once he did that he could use his shoulders and his hips to stay that single step ahead. He had what his coach started to think of as some sort of intangible "edge," a belief that he could play against anybody and everybody, and that belief, justified or not, seemed to turn contagious with his teammates.

They began to think they could play with opponents who were supposed to be better than they were.

So they did.

That summer, before his senior year of high school, Jason left an all-star camp in New Jersey early one morning and flew to a tournament in Louisville, Kentucky, where he joined up with his club team and played six games – that day.

He hit game-winning buzzer-beaters in three of them, two floaters near the basket and one jumper from deeper, and his team made it to the finals.

His teammates started putting the ball in his hands at the ends of games.

"He accepted that role," one of them would say later, "of 'I want the ball, I'll take the ball, we'll get what we want.'"

In October 2003, when Jason told the coaches he wanted to come to the school, McKillop sent him an e-mail. The coach was blunt with his assessment. He always is with recruits. He told Jason he made poor decisions with his shots. He told him he stood too much in "no man's land." He told him he saw the offense but didn't see the defense and made too many mistakes because of it. He went on.

"There's no time to relax," he wrote. "There's no time to take a breather. There's no time to think you have it made.

"Nor," the coach said, "is there time to think you can't make it."

Now with the Davidson fans in the stands in Detroit there was something like absolute faith in the team.

Earlier in the tournament, against Gonzaga, the team had come back from 11 points down in the second half. The team had come back from 17 down in the second half to beat Georgetown. The team had trailed Kansas by six *with less than a minute to go.*

So close, some had started to think.

But now anything seemed possible.

"Before every game in the tournament, they always seemed so hard, so unlikely, so insurmountable," student Lindsay Sween would say later, "but by that game, and within that moment, there was faith."

This was the feeling in Detroit. This was the thought back on campus inside the shoulder-to-shoulder student union and at the Brickhouse bar across Main Street in Davidson. This was the feeling at Providence Road Sundries in Charlotte and at Mercury Bar in Manhattan and at Fox and Hound in downtown Philadelphia and at Cheyenne Grill in Atlanta and at The Lion and Rose in San Antonio. This was the feeling 10 rows up from the bench at Ford Field.

Something good was about to happen.

This was new for Davidson basketball fans.

In 1994 the team had lost by a point in the Southern Conference championship game.

In 1996 the team had lost the conference championship game after going undefeated in the league in the regular season.

In 1998 the team had gotten to the NCAA tournament – for the first time with McKillop as the coach – but lost to Michigan in the first round.

In 2002 the team had gotten back to the NCAAs and in the first round against Ohio State had a lead in the second half but lost.

In 2006 the team went back and again had a lead in the second half. Lost.

Same thing in 2007.

Earlier in 2008, with the team that now had this chance against Kansas, there had been close losses to North Carolina, Duke and UCLA.

"Makes me so frustrated," Claire Asbury, the sophomore English major, wrote in her journal, "because I feel like we want to do it so badly and we just can never quite make it. But as Dad says 'keep the faith.'"

In January McKillop's team came back from six points down with three minutes to go to win against Elon. In February the team came back from 20 down in the first half to win against UNC Greensboro. And then came the tournament comebacks in March that made so many around the nation start watching. One fan said a timeout late in the game against Gonzaga had been what he considered a long-sought-after "moment of equilibrium." It wasn't a feeling of imminent victory. What it was, he said, was an overwhelming feeling of opportunity. The chance. *We can win this.* It was, for some alums, particularly for those who had been boys during the Lefty years of the 1960s, something like a reawakening of the possibility of national success. Two days after that, late in the second half of the comeback against Georgetown, one fan turned to his left and looked down his row in Raleigh and saw a white-haired alum with a single tear running down his cheek and then turned back to his young son and asked him to please watch this game close.

So now at Ford Field, a few rows behind the Davidson bench, Kerrin McKillop, the coach's daughter, Davidson Class of 2002, felt almost as if her team couldn't lose, and wouldn't.

"It sounds crazy," she would say later. "But I really felt like we almost couldn't be touched."

Stephen had done this.

Not just in this tournament, not even just during his sophomore season, but almost from the beginning, he had conditioned Davidson fans to start to think this way.

People around Davidson talked about the game at Greensboro, the 20-point comeback, when Stephen scored 41 points, 17 of them in less than six minutes in the second half.

But they also talked, still, about a game the year before, at home against UNC Greensboro, when Stephen was a freshman. And they talked about one play more than any other. Davidson had a tight six-point lead with 10 minutes left in the second half. Then Stephen hit a three-pointer from the right side. Then he ran back on defense and stole a long pass. Then he dribbled down the left sideline at a full sprint for about 50 feet with a defender running next to him. Then, all of a sudden, he stopped at the three-point line, the defender's momentum carried him past the baseline, and Stephen stepped back. Slow. Calm. And he swished another three. And the six-point lead was a 12-point lead, and it had happened in 12 seconds, and Stephen ran down the court toward the student section and smiled and stuck out his tongue and looked like a little boy.

After the game McKillop called it as magical a sequence as he had ever seen.

Those 12 seconds changed the tenor of the talk about basketball around the Davidson campus.

The crowds grew.

No one wanted to miss what the kid would do next.

Back in the spring of 1988, when Stephen was two weeks old, his mother took him to one of his father's NBA games when he was playing in Cleveland with the Cavaliers. Stephen slept in the car seat all the way to the game, he woke up and kept his eyes open for the whole game, and then after the game he closed them again when they got back to the car for the drive home.

A few years later, when Dell Curry was with the Charlotte Hornets, Sonya Curry sat with their son at the old Charlotte Coliseum.

"See your dad?"

Stephen watched his dad at games, practices, workouts in the summers. He rarely sat down. He didn't want to go to the concession stand. He watched in a way that was highly unusual. He didn't watch the ball. He watched his father, which meant he watched his father move mostly without the ball, and for 16 years in the NBA that meant he watched a world-class reader and user of screens.

ESPN analyst Jay Bilas says Stephen is one of the smartest players he has ever seen.

"Not in college. Period."

Now, though, Dell was the one watching Stephen.

In Stephen's freshman year, Dell was sitting in Charleston, watching the Southern Conference semifinals, when he saw Stephen do something that was new. Stephen was standing in the right corner. His defender was facing him with his back to the basket. Jason was bringing the ball up but he hadn't crossed half-court yet. And Stephen jerked his head to the left. Just his head. His defender lurched that way.

Dell turned to Sonya.

"It took me five years in the NBA," he told his wife, "before I could do that."

If Stephen could do that, Dell thought, if his defenders were giving him that amount of respect for his shot – if he could get his defenders to move without having to even move his own feet – he now could make them run into screens the way he wanted them to. He didn't have to simply respond to what *they* were doing. It was a subtle, even invisible thing for most people in the stands, but for Dell it was a sign of what was to come, or at least what could come.

In this 2008 NCAA tournament, Stephen had scored 30 points in the second half against Gonzaga, and another 25 in the second half against Georgetown. In that game, with less than four minutes to go, he had dribbled into the defense, past three defenders, and had scooped a shot high off the backboard and back down through the net. That gave Davidson a 62-60 lead, but it was what Stephen did on the next play that the Davidson coaches were thinking about in the huddle now on the Ford Field sideline.

Stephen had dribbled up the court, used a screen set near the top of the key and swished a 25-foot, wrist-flicked three-pointer with two Georgetown defenders running at him.

The lead was five.

The play was Flat.

What was amazing to veteran associate head coach Matt Matheny on the bench when that happened in the Georgetown game wasn't that the ball went in. It was that the flat ball screen created only the tiniest opening in which a shot was at all possible. The play didn't even work that well. And yet it still worked.

Stephen made it work.

Behind McKillop in the huddle at Ford Field was Max Paulhus Gosselin.

He was not one of the five Davidson players who was going to be on the court for the game's final play. The junior guard's specialty was his defense. Bryant Barr had checked in because the sophomore had a better jump shot. Still, though, Max now leaned over McKillop's left shoulder and looked at the coach's clipboard.

McKillop first had seen Max at an all-star camp in Atchison, Kansas, upstairs in a gym that was so hot the players had started to call it "the oven." Most of the players were sweating and sagging. But Max, 6-foot-6 and from the southern suburbs of Montreal, was running, jumping and diving on the floor.

The coach went to visit Max and his parents in Chambly, Quebec, and told his parents that he liked their son as a prospect because he could have an impact on a game without scoring a point. McKillop speaks very little French, and Max's parents don't speak that much English, but they communicated nonetheless. They connected. "When he touches you," Jean-Philippe Gosselin would say later, "you feel like part of the family."

Max doesn't watch sports on television. The only basketball games he watches are the ones he plays in. He spoke no English three years before he got to Davidson. He is one of the best students on the team, and he majors in sociology because he is fascinated by how people who are different try to get along.

Once Max was asked where his endless energy comes from.

He said his parents had started a cheese importing company and had built it into one of the largest in Canada. He said his father's father had had 11 children and worked 27 years treading tires in a Goodyear factory.

Lots of people work hard, Max said.

"Some people drill a hole 3,000 times a day, eight hours a day, their whole life," he said. "If someone can do that, why can't I give 100 percent, for 40 minutes, in a basketball game?

"I just try," he said.

To the left of Max in the huddle was Andrew Lovedale.

He had become a starter at forward after Christmas. Davidson had not lost since. His games in the tournament were his best yet. But he had fouled out late against Kansas and now he had to watch from the bench.

Andrew was born in Nigeria. He was the eighth of 10 children. He was 13 when his father died. He moved to England three years later because his older brother lived there and drove a bus in London. He trained in Manchester, England, at a basketball gym run by former NBA player John Amaechi. That's where McKillop first saw him. Andrew was sweeping the floor of the court, and with great care, McKillop thought, to get it ready for the younger kids he helped coach.

The kids there loved him.

"Kids know," Amaechi said. "If you're disingenuous, they know. There was no pretension about him. The thing that he did was he brought joy to the basketball center the moment he walked in the door.

"He is a unifying force."

Andrew brings old sneakers and basketballs back to Nigeria when he goes home in the summers. In the tournament against Gonzaga, toward the end of the game, he had sprinted to the right baseline to get a loose offensive rebound, then turned to whip a pass to Stephen, who hit a three-pointer that gave Davidson the lead. After the game, in the locker room, Andrew hugged his teammates, long embraces, and then sat quietly in front of his locker. He took a breath and bowed his head.

"God, I thank you," he whispered.

Now, on the other side of the huddle, Stephen looked at Bryant. They were roommates, had been from freshman orientation on, and they went to church together on Sunday mornings. Bryant was to be in the left corner for the play, and Stephen told him to be ready for the ball. Be ready to shoot. The referee's whistle sounded and the huddle started to break.

Steve Rossiter adjusted the waistband on his shorts and tightened the drawstring in front. Rossiter is from Staten Island and is the son of a retired New York City firefighter and a special-education teacher. He has the team's only visible tattoo.

It's on his right shoulder.

FEARLESS.

He was considered the second-best screen-setter on the team. Back in his senior year of high school, when McKillop went to watch him play,

Rossiter played one of his worst games. In the second half, he was sitting on the bench, and his backup scored. Rossiter stood up and cheered.

McKillop offered him a scholarship after the game.

Now Rossiter talked to teammate Thomas Sander.

Thomas was the best screen-setter on the team. Maybe the best McKillop had ever had. He turned to talk to Rossiter. Thomas' nickname on the team was the General, Rossiter's was the Colonel, and now the two of them decided that Thomas was going to be the one to set the flat screen at the top of the key.

In high school, at least for a time, Thomas considered not even playing basketball in college. He grew up in Cincinnati and attended Elder High, a Catholic, community service-oriented school on the city's hard-working west side. Thomas loved Elder, and his coach there. He was recruited by many Midwestern universities, but he didn't trust what those coaches were promising. He wanted to keep playing. He just wanted to find the right place to do that.

Davidson assistant coach Jim Fox went to Cincinnati to watch him play a game in early February. McKillop was there two weeks later.

Thomas could score, but what he loved was setting screens and taking charges – talents that box scores don't measure. He spent summer afternoons working on screening angles. In games his teammates huddled around him. He was the leader.

Earlier in his Davidson career, he had scored more, but that wasn't his role on the 2008 team. Now he anchored the defense. At the beginning of the season he had developed a cyst near his tailbone. In high school, he had played through injuries, and in college, too. Concussion. Bruised back. Reconstructed ankle. But the cyst was a problem because it made it almost unbearable to do what made him special. He couldn't take a charge. It hurt too much to hit the court with his butt. So the team doctor lanced the cyst. The team trainer used a sewing machine for the first time since junior high home economics class to turn some hard plastic and a football girdle into what all the players on the team started calling Thomas' butt pad.

Everything was fine until late in the first half of the tournament game against Gonzaga.

Thomas reached for a loose ball near the basket and jammed his right thumb. An X-ray just before halftime showed a break on the side of the tip of his thumb. The team doctor said the decision to play or not was up to Thomas. The decision was easy. Thomas was going to play. In a room off to the side, the doctor shot, with a .22-gauge needle, directly into the part of the bone that was broken, a mixture of numbing, fast-acting pain medications Ethyl Chloride, Marcaine and Lidocaine. Thomas looked away.

He came back into the main part of the locker room where his teammates had gathered for halftime. The coaches were still out in the hall. He had his thumb stuck in a cup of ice.

Jason Richards, his roommate and his best friend, looked up at him.

"Is it broken?" he asked.

"Yeah," Thomas said.

There was a short anxious silence in the room.

Davidson was down by five.

"Are you still going to play?" Jason said.

"Yeah," Thomas said.

He sat down. His teammates looked at him. All of them, he thought to himself, would do the same thing for him.

People close to the team knew about the injury, but most people did not, and the hope was that opponents wouldn't either.

"I'll be okay," Thomas told reporters who asked about it.

Thomas got the painkilling shots before the next three games in the tournament. They made his right hand so numb he sometimes had to look down at the ball to make sure he had gotten a rebound. And yet in the Kansas game, midway through the first half, he somehow had made a three-pointer with a hand he couldn't even feel.

Now McKillop watched his players leave the huddle and take the floor.

He was a different coach than the one who had come to Davidson in 1989 so intense and so self-assured.

"A changed man," one of his former players said.

"Changed completely," said another. "One-eighty."

Those who know him and have worked with him and have played for him say that over the last decade and a half he has become more relaxed, more mature as a coach, statesmanlike even. They say he's loosened up. They say he's more approachable and more comfortable with who he is. The cockiness is gone. What's left instead is confidence.

The old McKillop – the one who would make his players run sprint after sprint in the early morning dark and keep the heat off in the team bus after a loss – *that* McKillop used to play professors in lunchtime pickup games as if they were the NBA finals. He would play rough one-on-one in his gravel driveway against fans of the team. He would jab his elbow into a player's chest to test toughness. He would jam knives into locker room bulletin boards and tables in hotel ballrooms to teach killer instinct.

"He put pressure on you from the moment he saw you," one former player said.

The new McKillop, though, almost never lets one of his players come off the court in a game without a touch of the hand. This new coach tells his assistant coaches that the older he gets the more he cries. This new coach takes a ball that bounces to him out of bounds in a Sweet 16 game and dribbles it playfully through his legs before tossing it back to the referee. That had happened two nights before against Wisconsin, and had not gone unnoticed.

It wasn't as if McKillop was one way one day and another way the next. It was an evolution, not a flicked switch, but to try to change was a conscious decision he had made after that night in Anderson, South Carolina, in early March 1992.

"Maybe," he would say years later, "I had to go through that humbling experience and fail as miserably as I did to realize I was losing sight of what my mission was."

"When he became himself," said Jason Zimmerman, who was one of his first recruits at Davidson, "he started winning."

Back when Zimmerman was a high school recruit, McKillop had come to his house in Indiana and told him his vision for Davidson: *We're going to win there.* In 1994, when Zimmerman was a Davidson senior, the team finally was winning more – but he was playing less. It was a difficult lesson at the time.

McKillop gave him some handouts one day on the team bus that season.

The first handout was titled SOME REASONS WHY GOD DELAYS MEETING OUR NEEDS.

"God often waits," it said, "until we have come to the end of ourselves ..."

The second handout was titled ALL OUR ANXIETIES.

"Humble yourselves," it said, "under the mighty hand of God, that He may exalt you at the proper time ..."

Later that year, in the summer of 1994, Mark Donnelly had finished his freshman season at Davidson, and he was playing in a pro-am league near his home in New Jersey when he started playing out of control, getting upset at every little thing and cursing.

Mark's father was in the stands. Dave Donnelly had been half-expecting the outburst, and he took his son out into the parking lot.

"I'll get you help," he said.

When Mark was six, the family had been in Florida for vacation, and Mark went down a water park slide with his mother. She had a heart attack on the way down. Her body had to be pulled from the pool.

Mark used basketball as a way to cope. He played all the time, and played well, and was first-team all-state as a senior in New Jersey. He picked Davidson over Rutgers and Florida State. But all the accolades, it turned out, were distractions. His freshman year at Davidson was the first time he wasn't a star. Classes were a challenge. North Carolina was different from New Jersey. That summer he couldn't suppress his grief any longer.

Mark couldn't play the way he was. He needed to take a year off.

But he was worried about what McKillop might say. The best competitors, Mark thought, were tough. They played hurt. And the team at Davidson had just won more than 20 games for the first time with McKillop as coach. McKillop's program was on the rise, finally, and Mark was supposed to be an important part of it. The coaches were expecting big things. Mark was worried he might not be able to keep his scholarship when he called McKillop and told him what had happened with his mother, and what had happened in the summer league game, and what he had to do to feel right again.

That night on the phone, McKillop told him he could keep his scholarship – even, the coach said, if he never played basketball again.

The next morning, the doorbell rang at the Donnellys' home in Fairhaven, New Jersey.

Dave Donnelly opened the door.

Bob McKillop was standing there.

Around that time McKillop and his assistants started recruiting a promising guard from nearby North Mecklenburg High School named Titus Ivory.

They thought he could be the player who gave the program a boost. He was a winner. They recruited him hard when he was at North Mecklenburg and kept recruiting him hard even after he went to play a year at a prep school in Massachusetts in an effort to attract attention from schools with bigger programs. Titus Ivory liked Davidson and

McKillop, and his parents really liked Davidson and McKillop, but in the end he went to Penn State.

Two years after he made that decision, in April of 1998, Titus Ivory's dad died of a heart attack. The funeral was at Friendship Missionary Baptist Church in Charlotte. At the funeral, Terrell Ivory, Titus' younger brother, turned around and saw McKillop sitting in the upstairs balcony. The coach didn't need to be there, Terrell thought, especially after he had spent so much time recruiting Terrell's older brother to no avail. But there he was. Terrell decided he would go to Davidson if he could so he could try to play for McKillop. He did, and ended up making the team as a non-scholarship player. He was a captain his senior year.

"The day I lost my father," Terrell Ivory would say later, "was the day Coach McKillop sort of walked into my life. And every time I leave Davidson, he gives me a hug, and he says, 'I love you,' and it doesn't feel weird."

After the rainy night in Anderson, South Carolina, not everything changed. McKillop's thank-you notes still arrived with impeccable Catholic-school script. His tie was still tied with the perfect knot. He never looked like he needed a haircut, or that he had just gotten one. His typed-out practice plans still were to-the-minute specific. He still kept organized files of those practice plans, from every day, from every year. And the glow of the light in his office still could be seen from the Baker Sports Complex parking lot late at night. Over the years, though, longtime fans started seeing McKillop smile more at the ends of timeouts. He was, they thought, a little more human.

He started trusting his assistant coaches more.

His players started seeing more of what one would call the "hand-across-your-back" McKillop.

In 2005, the team went undefeated in the Southern Conference, and in the locker room before the semifinals in the conference tournament he told his players there was no reason to feel pressure.

No pressure, he kept saying.

He said the word so many times, though, it was clear to Thomas Sander that McKillop was feeling plenty of pressure. The team lost the game and ended up with no spot in the NCAAs.

The next year he hardly mentioned the word.

After a loss on the road late that season, McKillop walked to the back of the bus, where his players were sitting. They braced for hollering.

"We're okay," he told them. "Lesson learned."

A couple weeks after that Davidson won the conference tournament to get back to the NCAAs.

And in 2008, in January, two months before the Kansas game, McKillop gave a speech at a dinner on campus celebrating 100 years of Davidson basketball. With many of his former players sitting there he apologized to them for not having been better sooner.

He told his team throughout the NCAA tournament run that he felt at peace. He felt at ease, he told them, because they had put him at ease.

In his news conferences during the tournament, he talked about the importance of caring, and showing it, and about the importance of balance. "Our system," he said, "is based on balance." Between fearlessness and patience. Between freedom and discipline. Between humility and confidence.

"I'm at ease now in my life," he told reporters in Detroit. "I have never been more at ease, more comfortable, more grounded than where

I am right now.

"I think," he said, "it's a response to the pursuit of something and seeing it happening right in front of your eyes, knowing the investment, and realizing how many people were part of this investment, and now sharing in this investment."

Now, watching in a basement bar in Rumson, New Jersey, was Mark Donnelly.

Mark thought about that morning in 1994 when McKillop showed up at his door. He thought about his senior year in 1998 when his team helped get McKillop to the NCAAs for the first time. He thought about the call he made after the Georgetown win earlier in the tournament. McKillop answered while he was on the bus home from Raleigh. Waiting for him in Davidson were toilet-papered trees and bed-sheet signs made with red and black spray paint and hung on people's porches. Over the phone Mark could hear McKillop's smile.

Watching from a few rows behind the bench in Detroit was Terrell Ivory. He was standing and holding his breath.

And down the row from him was Jason Zimmerman.

Zimmerman thought back to 2007. He had lost his job as an assistant coach at the University of Evansville and drove all the way from Indiana down to Davidson because he felt the need to be home. He walked into the Davidson team's locker room and saw a message written on a piece of paper stuck to the bulletin board.

He wrote it down: "Search for success and you will find emptiness. Search how you can help people and you will find success. You can get anything you want if you help others get what they want."

Before a game in Detroit, he had given McKillop an envelope, and in that envelope was a note.

"A great man gave me these 14 years ago," the note read. "They ring true today."

In the envelope were the handouts from 1994.

Higher up in the stands in Detroit was a man named Randy Lawrence.

Lawrence was 57 and had moved to the town of Davidson back in 1993 and met McKillop early on. He heard the coach speak at Davidson College Presbyterian Church. Lawrence wasn't a Davidson grad, and he wasn't a big basketball fan, but he had taken his three children to games when they were young.

Recently, though, Lawrence had been having a rough time.

He lost his mother in 2003.

He got divorced after that.

He was drinking a lot, and his loneliness was making it worse.

He had bought season tickets to the basketball games and joined the booster club mainly to get out of the house and to see some people he knew. He watched McKillop from his seat at Belk Arena.

On Christmas Eve in 2007, Randy's children were gone, his house was empty, and he was alone.

The phone rang.

It was McKillop.

"Merry Christmas," the coach said.

At that time McKillop's team had a record of four wins and six losses.

"If you need anything," the coach said, "just call."

Lawrence thanked McKillop and hung up. But he was puzzled. Why would the basketball coach call him? Why would the basketball coach call him *on Christmas Eve*? Lawrence figured there was something McKillop had seen, or sensed, and he was humbled by that.

A week went by.

New Year's Day.

Lawrence was struggling, again, alone in an empty house. He had been trying to control his drinking. He felt helpless and didn't know what else to do. All he knew was that he had to change. So he called the basketball coach who had called him.

"I need help," Lawrence said.

McKillop told him to get closer to God.

"But I need to hold onto something right now," Lawrence said.

"I'm sorry," McKillop said. "That's all I can tell you."

Lawrence hung up again.

But he went to church the next Sunday at Davidson United Methodist Church, and the Sunday after that, and the Sunday after that.

He joined a singles group.

He stopped drinking.

And he started going to more basketball games. He watched McKillop and his players. He watched how they sacrificed their own egos for the good of the team. He watched how so many of the players' parents came to so many of the games. The players couldn't do it alone, he thought, and neither could McKillop – and neither could he. After games, the players came toward the fans in the stands and waved to *them* and clapped for *them* to thank them for coming. McKillop and his players, Lawrence felt, were cheering for him as much as he was cheering for them.

This team, Lawrence said, was ministering to him. All of this, at least for him, had become something like a spiritual experience.

He started making trips to away games. He went to Charleston, South Carolina, for the Southern Conference tournament. He went to Raleigh and to Detroit for the games in the NCAAs.

Now, here at the end, with Davidson down by just two points, with the players taking the floor, with more than 57,000 people cheering for the players who had cheered for him, he stood up with tears in his eyes and looked down at McKillop near the bench.

McKillop, Lawrence believed, had done something remarkable on Christmas Eve. The phone needed to ring, and it did, and it was McKillop. The coach, he thought, had made the right call at the right time.

Now Stephen walked from the huddle and along the sideline. Written in neat black print on the side of his left red and white Nike was "I can do all things …" It was a reference to Philippians 4:13: "I can do all things through Christ who gives me strength." Earlier in the season, written on his shoe was Romans 8:28: "And we know that in all things God works for the good of those who love Him, who have been called according to

His purpose." Stephen's not an evangelist. The scripture on his shoes is meant only to be a reminder for him. Now, at about half-court, still on the sideline, he made a fist with his right hand and hit his chest by his heart and then pointed with his index finger up high.

Stephen points a lot on the court, to his teammates when they pass him the ball, to the fans in the stands. Against Gonzaga, in the tournament, he hit a three-pointer with a minute to go in the game, and he pointed to his father in the front row, the way Dell Curry used to point at his father many years ago. That's Stephen. He takes the praise and he tries to turn it around. He tries to widen the spotlight.

His teammates feel that. Andrew Lovedale described the attention Stephen was getting as family wealth. If your brother is rich, he explained, you're rich, too.

Earlier in the year, Lovedale, a junior, had replaced Boris Meno, a senior, in the starting lineup. It was a difficult decision for McKillop and the other coaches, who were concerned that Meno might be discouraged and that his contributions could wane. But before every game, Stephen started coming over to the bench, before the tip, and giving Boris a hug. The coaches noticed the gesture immediately, and its importance.

In February, after a win in the last home game of the season in which Jason Richards had been honored for his four years at Davidson and then scored the 1,000th point of his career, the SportSouth television network wanted to do an interview with Stephen.

He said no.

"This," he said, "is Jason's day."

In March, after the win over Georgetown, Stephen made a five-minute appearance on ESPN's Pardon The Interruption, the popular sports talk show. He ended the interview by holding up a big shot of Jason's face in front of his face and playfully acting out the role of an overlooked star. The hosts laughed. To those who knew Davidson, though, and to those who knew Stephen, it was no meaningless goof.

Stephen was asked in a news conference during the tournament what his "secret" was.

No secret, he said.

"Our system here," he said. "It's nothing special that I do. I just get screens from Andrew and Thomas and other big guys down low. Our assists man, he's great at being patient and finding guys when they're open. So when I'm open I get the ball …"

"Nothing special I'm doing," he said again.

Waiting for Stephen and Jason and their teammates now on the Ford Field floor were the Kansas Jayhawks. They were a top seed in the tournament. They had four McDonald's All-Americans. They had four players who were 6-foot-9 or taller. They had five players who in three months would be drafted by NBA teams. They had won 34 times in 37 games. They had as a program won more games than all but two teams in the history of college basketball.

How had this happened?

How had Davidson played this Kansas team so well, with the score 59-57 this late in the game, now with the ball and a chance to win?

The coach of the team had grown up a skinny-necked altar boy in South Ozone Park, Queens, just off Rockaway Boulevard, in a working-class neighborhood in a small row house with a low concrete stoop.

McKillop was the fourth-shortest boy in his First Communion class of 90 in the parish of Our Lady of Perpetual Help.

He wore the same green coat and black tie every day to Chaminade High School because there was a dress code and because his father was a city cop and city cops made what they made. He worked at church bingo and delivered groceries to earn the tuition his parents couldn't afford.

He was cut from the freshman basketball team. He was cut from the junior varsity team as a sophomore. He was cut from the varsity team as a junior. But he still played in church youth leagues and on the courts at Prospect Park in East Meadow on Long Island. He played more than just about anybody in his neighborhood, and finally he made varsity as a senior. He started only one game in high school, and yet he played college basketball at East Carolina and Hofstra, where he was the team MVP in 1972. He earned an NBA tryout after his senior year.

For Davidson, he recruits, at least one former player thought, players who remind him of *him.*

Too small. Too slow.

Overlooked.

And then he gets players like that to play together.

Back in the middle of the 1980s McKillop gave a lecture at the summer basketball camp he ran at Long Island Lutheran High School. He brought props: thin wood paint-stirring sticks.

He called a boy out of the bleachers and gave him one of the sticks.

"Break it," he told the boy.

The boy broke it.

He gave the boy two sticks stacked together.

"Break them," he told the boy.

The boy broke them.

Then he gave the boy five sticks stacked together.

"Break them," he told the boy.

The boy tried. He could not.

One five, McKillop believed, even back then, is harder to break than five ones.

"Everything we do," the coach once wrote in a handout he gave to his team, "will be dictated by 5 guys doing it together. We will never tolerate only 4 guys doing it or only 3 guys doing it. Every possession, offense or defense, 5 guys will be working together."

"Our five guys," Max Paulhus Gosselin once said, "against your five guys."

Davidson basketball over McKillop's 19 years has come to mean many things. Those things are passed from class to class. Little things aren't little things. Have no fear of physical contact. Finish.

"Attack the attacker," McKillop tells them.

When we win, he says, Davidson wins.

They run a motion offense, patient but not slow, "reads" rather than sets. It's a system that demands synched-up, quick-thinking players instead of trained, rote runners. Sharp passes. Precise cuts. Stout screens.

On defense, they emphasize no easy dribbles, no easy passes, all-out effort all the time. And maybe the most important of all tasks: Do not let the man with the ball get into the middle near the basket.

"They're the opposite of any stereotype I think people place on them," Texas coach Rick Barnes once said. "People look at them as smart white kids, and they think maybe they're not that athletic. They're much more athletic than you might think. They're not going to pound their chests but inside the belly's boiling and they want to smack you in the mouth."

"A lot of times you get fighters who aren't good kids or good kids who aren't fighters," former North Carolina coach Matt Doherty said. McKillop, Doherty believed, has "good kids who are fighters."

That, maybe, was why 13.6 million people were watching now on CBS. Stephen was part of the draw. A big part. But why were sports writers saying it would be better for the *world* if Davidson won this game?

Davidson players are trained to know where their opponents are weak. Where they can be beaten. That isn't unusual.

But they also are taught to be sufficiently self-critical to know where they themselves are weak. That *is* unusual. Especially in the mostly macho culture of sports. The key: To know one's weaknesses is the first step to turning those weaknesses into strengths.

Opposing coaches talk about how Davidson pushes the pace on offense. They talk even more about how they push the pace the hardest right after an opponent *makes* a basket. The players practice not even letting the ball hit the floor. Take it straight out of the net, pass it to the point guard – go, go, go. It is, for Davidson coaches and players, a conscious decision to not dwell, even for an instant, on the bad thing, and to try to turn it into a good thing. But it is also an understanding that the other team's players probably will relax after making a basket. They don't need to make an egregious show of celebration. Even just a fist pump or a "Yes!" Inside that tiny moment is weakness, and inside that weakness is opportunity for McKillop's team.

The Davidson coaches also don't call dead-ball situations dead-ball situations. Those are out-of-bounds plays, free throws, anything where the clock is stopped. They call these plays "special teams." "Dead balls" connotes time to rest, and there's no time to rest. Opponents' hands on knees, hands on waists, the catching of breath: Those are opportunities, too.

They practice these things. They "simulate" actions that happen over and over in games. Tapping out offensive rebounds. Saving loose balls near the sideline. Running over to McKillop for timeouts. A bed, one former player once said, doesn't get made military-style just once. The idea is to develop habits.

McKillop's teams also try to play Duke nearly every season, and North Carolina as often as possible, and also North Carolina State. Anybody who is going to make them better.

"Sometimes," McKillop once said, "you don't learn lessons from winning. Sometimes you learn lessons from losing."

Davidson has time to do that.

Not every team does.

Kansas had a sophomore and two juniors who were going to leave for the NBA. That has become the norm for the best players on the best college teams in today's step-skipping culture. Potential is rewarded sometimes more than production. But Davidson had a senior point guard. Davidson had senior forwards. Davidson had a coach with almost 20 years of experience at the same place. McKillop had players who almost always played their best toward the ends of their careers. And his teams almost always played their best at the ends of seasons. Even when his teams weren't very good, they finished, and finished well.

The 2008 team had started the season with six losses in its first 10 games. Now they were 16.8 seconds and a three-point shot away from their 26th straight win, and the Final Four. They had not lost in the calendar year.

In Detroit a reporter had asked McKillop about his team's 4-6 start.

"We did not surrender," McKillop said.

"Our world today is full of surrender: People surrender morals, principles, beliefs, dreams, at the first sign of a challenge, at the first sign of failure.

"We did not surrender," he said again.

Against Kansas, in the last minute of the game, his team had been down 59-53.

But Davidson got an offensive rebound off a free throw situation.

An out-of-bounds play led to a free throw made.

A second out-of-bounds play led to a three-pointer from Stephen.

It was 59-57, one last defensive possession left for Davidson, and in that possession Jason slid his feet to his right and strained to keep a Kansas guard from getting into the middle. *Do not let the man with the ball get into the middle.* The Kansas guard had to pass the ball back outside.

"Crisco" did that.

Months later, William Robertson, Davidson Class of 1975 and the chaplain at the state mental hospital in Morganton, North Carolina, would wonder whether people aren't somehow hard-wired to be attracted to stories that contain moments like this. They tell a truth in the end.

From struggle comes patience. From patience comes experience.

From experience comes hope.

And hope?

Hope does not disappoint.

That, he said, is the theology of the cross. It's Romans 5.

Now, in Morganton, he sat with his mother in the den of her home. This was where he had watched Davidson's regional final games against North Carolina in 1968 and 1969. His dad had gone to Davidson in the 1940s and played on the basketball team. William pulled for Davidson growing up. Just before high school he moved from nearby Hendersonville to Morganton.

The games in '68 and '69 mattered to him.

The kids who were the Carolina fans were the cheerleaders. They were the football players. They were the kids who had the right clothes.

William was a Davidson fan.

He was awkward and shy.

If Davidson won, he thought back then, he wouldn't have to feel that way anymore.

Davidson lost the game in 1968 by four points.

Davidson lost the game in 1969 by two points.

William went to Davidson and then on to Harvard Divinity School. In his time in Boston he followed the Red Sox and was at Fenway Park in 1978 when the rival Yankees won that year's one-game playoff.

This was how he came to see sports. The experience of caring about a team existed to examine how people dealt with disappointment and defeat.

After that Red Sox game his mother gave him a letter that the poet Emily Dickinson had written to a friend in 1880.

"I trust your Garden was willing to die," the poet wrote. "I do not think that mine was – it perished with beautiful reluctance, like an evening star – I hope you were well since we knew of you, and as happy as Sorrow would allow.

"There are Sweets of Pathos," Dickinson wrote, "when Sweets of Mirth have passed away."

William thought a lot about that letter.

He thought a lot about loss and what it meant and what to do with that.

Now, in the den of his mother's home, he was 55, living there because he had split from his wife with whom he has three children, caring for his ailing 81-year-old mother, bringing her groceries and getting her mail, and going to work at a mental hospital where people were asking hard questions about worth and value and what life is truly about. He had come to believe that the only difference between him and the people he worked with was a safety net. If a person can't strive and then fail, he thought, that person can't be healthy.

"Because ultimately," the chaplain said, "*ultimately*, you don't get to the top of the mountain. But you have to be able to risk. You have to be able to take that chance. You have to be able to live that moment.

"You have to be able to throw it up there," he said, "knowing that it'll be okay if it doesn't go in."

Now, in the stands in Detroit, Cate Bell, a Davidson alum who used to be a student manager for the team, stood up and then sat back down. She writes McKillop a longhand letter after every season thanking him for his ongoing role at her school. He writes back thanking *her*. Now she closed her eyes. She had seen these sorts of last-minute situations work well in practice drills. She opened her eyes and stood back up and put her hands on the back of the seat in front of her.

Jennifer Matheny, the wife of associate head coach Matt Matheny, sat with Brock, their young son. He was three, almost four, and he gets frightened by loud noise. She had gotten him little red earplugs and they had worked. But now the noise in Ford Field was too much, and Brock started to cry. Jennifer Matheny sat down and held her son.

Up about 25 rows, Tripp Cherry, a 1999 Davidson grad, called his wife, Carrie, Class of 2001. They have Davidson season tickets and often make road trips to games, but she was back home in Charlotte studying for law school exams. Now they talked on the phone about this play that was about to happen.

"Hey," she said. "I should let you go."

"No," he said. "Stay."

McKillop watched his players take their spots on the court. Stephen passed the ball inbounds to Rossiter, Rossiter passed it back to Stephen, and Stephen started to dribble up the court.

In the summer of 1989, when Bob and Cathy McKillop moved their own family from Merrick, New York, to North Carolina, their children Kerrin, Matt and Brendan were nine, six and almost one. They drove down, the five of them, in their blue Volvo station wagon with Brendan in his car seat in the middle in the back. Kerrin and Matt didn't want to go.

"Many tears," Cathy McKillop remembered.

Kerrin at first hated living in Davidson. It was hot. People talked funny and slow. The new house on Concord Road across from campus didn't smell like home. The school she went to wasn't a Catholic school and the church on the corner wasn't a Catholic church. But she wanted to go to the church on the corner. Everybody else went to the church on the corner.

"Why," she asked her dad, "can't we go to the church on the corner?"

"Because we're different," her dad said.

That was 19 years ago.

McKillop could have left Davidson in 1994. Hofstra, his alma mater, was looking for a new coach, but he pulled his name out of the search. He had just been to his first Southern Conference championship game with Davidson.

He could have left in 1998. He came close to getting the job at St. John's. He interviewed twice but St. John's hired Mike Jarvis for seven years and $5 million. McKillop had just been to his first NCAA tournament with Davidson.

He could have left in 1999. He almost took the job at Stony Brook University. The athletic director there was a close friend, and he received a multi-year, six-figure offer. McKillop considered it so strongly that he actually resigned from Davidson on a Wednesday before changing his mind on a Friday. Kerrin had just finished her freshman year at Davidson.

When it had come time for Kerrin to pick a college, she got into Duke, Georgetown and Notre Dame. Her parents wanted her to go to Notre Dame and made that clear. Her mother even sent the deposit to

Notre Dame. Kerrin wanted to go to Davidson.

Now, in Detroit behind the bench, she was four months from getting married to a Davidson man in Davidson College Presbyterian Church.

The church on the corner.

This was the McKillop parable: He came to Davidson to go somewhere else and ended up finding a home. Davidson became his home because it had become his family's home.

Cathy McKillop once put it like this: "We live in a place where our kids want to come home."

Sitting in the same row as Kerrin now in Detroit was her brother Matt. Matt went to Davidson, Class of 2006, and played on the team. And sitting on the bench was their brother Brendan. Brendan was a freshman on the team.

Matt's decision to go to Davidson had been different from Kerrin's because he wanted to play. But the coach wasn't sure his son was good enough. He wasn't sure it was a good idea even if he was. He called other coaches he knew who had coached their sons.

In the spring of 2002, when Matt was trying to decide on his college plans, after Davidson won the Southern Conference tournament, McKillop asked Matt to ride the team bus home from Charleston. He wanted him to know what it felt like to be on the bus on the trip home after clinching a bid to the NCAA tournament.

Brendan was on the bus too.

"Do you know what this means?" Matt's younger brother said.

"It means Dad wants you to play for him."

In his career at Davidson, Matt started almost 100 games, he hit over 200 threes, and in his senior year, in the quarterfinals of the

Southern Conference tournament, he led the team to a comeback win against The Citadel. Two days later Matt and the team were on their way to the NCAAs as league champions. He stood on the sideline near the end of that game using a towel to wipe tears from his eyes.

During his four years he brought his friends home with him for dinners. Many of his friends were his father's players. The coach had had his players over for dinners before, but now some of the players on his team had become like members of his family. Matt became a liaison for the players to the head coach in a way that before had been impossible.

At the gym, McKillop asked so much of his own son, and the other players noticed that, which meant he could ask so much of them.

All of them, McKillop started to say, were like his sons.

It was, said Cathy McKillop, one of the great gifts of his life.

With Stephen, earlier in the 2008 season, there had been a moment where he got hit in the nose and was bleeding. McKillop called him over and took a white handkerchief out of the right pocket of his suit pants and wiped the blood from Stephen's upper lip, quickly and gently, and then put the handkerchief back in his pocket.

Now in Detroit he stood on the sideline and watched Stephen approach half-court.

Jason Richards was in the right corner behind the three-point line being covered by Kansas guard Sherron Collins. Bryant Barr was in the left corner behind the three-point line being covered by Kansas guard

Russell Robinson. Stephen Rossiter was on the left low block near the basket being covered by Kansas forward Darrell Arthur. And Thomas Sander was on the right low block near the basket being covered by Kansas guard Mario Chalmers.

Now Thomas started to run toward the top of the key to set the flat ball screen for Stephen.

In Washington, D.C., B.J. Rudell, Davidson Class of 1995, sat alone in his apartment in front of his 42-inch DVR-equipped TV. The ball was about to be passed in, the play was about to start, and he realized he wasn't ready for any of this. He wasn't ready for a shot to miss, and he also wasn't ready for a shot to go in. Because what happens when a dream stops being a dream and all of a sudden it turns real?

So he picked up his remote.

And he hit pause.

Now Stephen crossed half-court. Kansas coach Bill Self had put in the game four guards and only one post player. Stephen was being guarded by 6-foot-6 Kansas star Brandon Rush.

There were nine seconds left.

McKillop said once that Stephen had given him a sense of peace as a coach. A kind of calm he had never felt. "He is someone," he said, "who can magically create opportunities for us to win."

Now Stephen dribbled toward Thomas.

Thomas set the flat ball screen on Rush.

Rush started to fall to the floor. Stephen darted to the left.

Now there were seven seconds left.

Jason was in the right corner. He watched Stephen stop going to his left and turn and start heading to his right and toward Thomas' second screen near the top of the key.

Six seconds.

Jason watched Chalmers duck past Thomas and chase Stephen, and he watched Rush get up off the floor and start chasing Stephen, too.

Five seconds.

Jason decided he had to move, because he didn't want this game to end with him just standing there, and if he stayed in the corner he would be doing nothing. He didn't want to be watching.

He wanted to help.

Jason started running toward Stephen.

Four seconds.

Stephen pump-faked and Rush jumped up and off to the side. Maybe here was a sliver of an opening for a shot. But Jason's defender was running after Jason and left him now and bolted toward Stephen. He had his arms straight up.

The opening had closed.

Three seconds.

Stephen had only one option.

Watching this now in the student union back in Davidson was history professor Sally McMillen.

She was Jason's thesis advisor. Jason reminded her of her own son. Blair McMillen is a concert pianist in New York, and Jason was one of her students, but they had the same shade of short brown hair and similar soft smiles and self-effacing senses of humor.

McMillen had seen in *The New York Times* the morning of the Wisconsin game a story about players and their moments in the NCAA tournament. Bill Bradley, the former senator who had played at Princeton and once scored 58 points in a tournament game, was quoted: "This is their moment in the sun, and it will be something they treasure for the rest of their lives. It's an identification with a particular player at a particular time, and the person who's going to remember it most is the player."

Bradley caught himself.

"The player and his mother."

McMillen had never met Jason's mother. But she clipped the story and looked up the Richards' home address in a college directory and stuck it in the mail.

McMillen once had asked Jason if he ever got nervous before big games. He said he did but that he was fine once he got out there onto the court. Then he could just play. McMillen thought of her son. Sometimes, her son said, he was nervous before a performance, but once he got out there, onto center stage, seated at the piano, the nervousness slipped away once his fingers touched the keys.

Now McMillen watched Stephen pass the ball to Jason. Jason was about 25 feet from the basket, far behind the three-point line, to the right of the center of the court.

Two seconds.

She watched the ball hit Jason's hands.

She watched the ball leave Jason's hands.

One second.

Oh Jason, she thought.

In Washington, B.J. Rudell, the Class of 1995 Davidson grad who had paused the DVR on his television, was thinking about how he had painted his face for the 1994 Southern Conference championship game that Davidson lost by one point on a missed shot at the buzzer. He was thinking about how he and his good friend that year had gone up to West Virginia to watch the team play and how McKillop and some of the players had thanked them for coming. He thought about the e-mail he had sent to the coach in late 2002 thanking him for what he had done for his 1,700-student college.

"Dear B.J.," McKillop had written back.

"Thanks so much for your very kind words. I hope that we can continue to represent Davidson in a way that makes every alum very proud. Although our record is 7-3, with 2 losses being to #1 Duke and #4

Arizona and the 3rd one being to a talented Florida State team, our players and our coaches are far from content with what we've accomplished to date. We also refuse to accept that this is a rebuilding year. Last May, 5 seniors graduated, and all 5 earned a championship, a diploma, and a professional basketball contract. I've challenged this year's 3 seniors to reach the same standard of excellence.

"Please know," McKillop wrote, "how much I appreciate your very kind words."

Now B.J. thought about the previous 10 days. He thought about the win over Gonzaga, and the win over Georgetown, and the win over Wisconsin. He thought about all the stories in the news from all over the country about his alma mater. "The face of this NCAA tournament." "The Wizard of Oz in short pants." "… story of the year in college basketball. Maybe of the decade. … Maybe several decades." "… a message for the world." And he thought about the text message he had gotten that week from a fellow Davidson alum.

"It's like a dream," it had said.

But now he looked at his cell phone.

It hadn't buzzed.

It was still, and it was silent, and Rudell knew. He unpaused his television. Not to see what had happened but to see how.

Jason had let the ball go with 1.3 seconds to go. A camera's flash went off in the stands near the basket with 1.1 seconds to go. Another went off in the second deck with 0.6 seconds to go. Jason started falling backwards with 0.3 seconds to go. There was a flash midway up the lower level of the stands, and then another, and then another. Jason put both hands up to cover his face. He hit the floor, first with his butt, then with his back. He folded his arms over his eyes. Bryant Barr was the first to get to him. Steve Rossiter was next. Then Thomas Sander after that. They helped him up. *Don't let a teammate stay down on the floor*: part of trust, commitment, care. Jason got up and leaned over and put his hands on his knees. He untucked his jersey and started to walk off the court and down a tunnel and back to the locker room.

He heard the crowd.

"Great run!"

"Head up!"

Back in Davidson, at the student union, with thousands of people packed in its rooms, first there had been silence.

But then there was clapping.

And then there was more.

The locker room was silent.

Max sat on the thin gray carpet in front of his locker in his sock feet. Stephen sat at the end of a row of chairs and stared at the floor. Jason sat to his left and had his head in his hands and McKillop put his right hand on the top of his head and held it there.

"We had a chance," Jason said in the news conference. "Maybe you could say we could have got a better shot. At that point it seemed the best shot for us."

Back in the lobby of the team hotel, before the team's flight home, Lindsay Richards was waiting to see her brother.

"We were in the lobby of the hotel after the game when we saw him," she would say later. "He came in on the bus. We were already there. Jason has always been a fighter. ... He's pretty good at bouncing back from things. But because this was such a bigger scale you just don't know. So he came in. And everyone was clapping. And he walked straight to my dad. Rarely do my dad and my brother cry. My dad held his head on his shoulder. And when Jason pulled away, his eyes were watering, and my dad's were, too. I didn't go to him for a while. I just watched. I didn't want to be crying when I went to him. I wanted to be stronger. I didn't want to be the sister who was tugging on him. So he came over to me. I was on the other side of the room. He came to me, and he gave me a hug, a bear hug, and he said: 'Are you crying?' I said no. He said: 'Why are you crying?' He said: 'Come on. Stop it. Stop crying.'

"'There's still more.'

"That's what he said.

"'There's still more.'"

In New York, late, Peter Anderer, the slow-footed former player who ended up as the Southern Conference tournament MVP in 2002, walked from the restaurant where he worked at 25th Street and Madison Avenue some 100 blocks all the way back to his place on Manhattan's Upper West Side. Someone at the restaurant had told him Davidson had lost by two. But he had recorded the game and he watched it when he got home. When it neared the end, he would say later, he knew Davidson hadn't won, he *knew* that, and he sat there and he watched, and he still thought his team was going to win.

"I still wasn't afraid."

Two days later, William Robertson, the chaplain at the Morganton mental hospital, sat in his small, cluttered office in the basement of Lippard Chapel and started to write for the fan forum at DavidsonCats.com.

"I've seen some pictures of Stephen Curry since Sunday, and he has been smiling," Robertson wrote. "I haven't seen any pictures of Jason Richards, but I hope he's smiling also. Because the last play of that great game was a very good play. It was probably the perfect play."

He wrote that McKillop trusted his players.

And that Stephen trusted Jason by passing him the ball.

And that Jason trusted that he still would be loved, even if he missed.

He quoted Faulkner, from *Intruder in the Dust*, about moments with so much to lose and so much to gain.

He thought about Davidson's moment.

"In that moment," he wrote, "we had in our hearts and minds, proleptically I think the theologians would say, the joy of having it go in. Before it was not in, it was as good as in. For that fraction of a second, we had that experience, and it is enough. It is well worth the journey. At least for me it is, and I guess the ultimate point of this too-long post is that I hope it is also worth it for Jason. He took the shot. He gave us that moment. He trusted, and all we can do is be sure our reaction is worthy of that trust."

It made people cry.

It made people preach.

It made people ask questions.

"What was it?"

"What was I watching?"

"What is winning?"

It made one man ask his son: "With what would you have been satisfied?"

"I don't know," the boy said. "I just didn't want it to end."

And it made people say things like this:

"We found something we didn't know we had lost."

"We're all seeking it. We're all wanting it. And there it was."

EPILOGUE

On a Tuesday evening in April Bob McKillop stood on a stage set up on the court at Belk Arena in front of thousands of fans still wanting all of it not to be over. He stood in front of his players seated in chairs on the stage and he turned to talk to them.

"The arena's going to empty out," the coach said. "The lights are going to be turned off. You're going to go back to your rooms. And in the silence of your rooms you're going to think about this particular night and think about this season and then you're going to wake up and understand that you lived this season with a dedication to commit yourselves to excellence. You lived this season with a dedication to commit yourselves to care for each other as teammates and you lived this season trusting each other, trusting yourselves, trusting your coaches – in good times and in bad – to do the right thing.

"Headlines are going to fade. Trophies? They're going to tarnish. But the relationships you have built this year, built upon trust, care and commitment, will last for your lifetimes."

He turned back around and faced the crowd.

"You can go to any library in America," he said, "you can go to any bookstore, and find row after row and shelf after shelf of self-help books. How to get better. How to live your life correctly. I've read many. But I come back always to one of the great books of all time.

"The Bible. Micah. Chapter 6."

He paused.

"Act justly," he said.

"Love tenderly.

"Walk humbly with your God."

The thousands of people broke the silence and clapped and clapped and then they stopped and it was silent again.

"That's the challenge that we now face," McKillop told the people. "We are an elite team. We are on a pedestal. We are on the Broadway stage.

"We need your prayers. We need your support. We need your help. We need your guidance.

"We need you," he said, "to hold us accountable as we continue to chase our dreams."

On a Thursday evening in May, at the team's annual year-end banquet, Jason Richards stood behind a podium in front of hundreds of fans sitting at tables arranged under a huge tent outside. He gave his senior speech. He talked about his four years at Davidson and on the team, and he started to cry.

"Sorry," he said.

There was silence.

A voice finally came from near the rear of the tent.

"Don't be sorry."

ACKNOWLEDGMENTS

I learned from doing this project what Davidson basketball players have learned for a long time from Bob McKillop.

You can't do it alone.

Bill Stevens and Neil Brown at the *St. Petersburg Times* gave me three months off to do this.

Bob McKillop, Matt Matheny and the rest of the Davidson family welcomed me back. The place felt like home 10 years ago, and still feels like home now.

I want to thank Bill Cobb, Jason and Traci Zimmerman, Will and Erica Roberson, Sally and Bruce McMillen, Terry and Beth Egan, Matt McKillop and Peyton Gallagher, Wes Goldsberry and Bro Krift for giving me places to stay along the way. The McMillens in particular contributed so many things to this project, but offering up their home for most of the summer is at the top of that very long list.

Many people read drafts and offered feedback. I especially want to thank Ben Montgomery, Tom Lake, Bro Krift, Terry Egan, William Robertson, Shary Lyssy Marshall and Meg and Chip Clark. Meg and Chip became friends through this effort. So did Eddie Nicholson. So did William Robertson. So did Bill Cobb. I'm grateful for that.

Thanks also to Bill Duryea, the national editor back in St. Pete, who toward the end, when it was most necessary, went above and beyond giving his time and working his magic.

And Meghan Martin.

She is my partner and my reason.

INTERVIEWS

I talked to these people in reporting for this project:

Harper Addison. John Akers. Tom Allen. Chris Alpert. John Amaechi. Peter Anderer. Scott Applegate. Germain Archambault. Will Archambault. Mike Aresco. Billy Armstrong. Claire Asbury. Tim Austing. Todd Babington. Erin Balak. Robert Banta. Rick Barnes. Dick Barney. Wendell Barnhouse. Bryant Barr. Don Barr. Susan Barr. Duggar Baucom. Bob "Butch" Beard. Susan Reid Beard. Joey Beeler. Cate Bell. John Bell. Ray Beltz. Rick Bender. Matt Berman. Jay Bilas. Eric Blancett. Aaron Bond. Eric Bossi. Nathan Bradshaw. Tina Bridgers. Will Brinson. Shonn Brown. Stan Brown. Will Bryan. John Bryant. Kimberly Bunting. David Burns. John Burns. Chris Burton. Jeff Bzdelik. Wes Calton. Zach Calucchia. Clark Candler. Laura Candler. Robbie Carnegie. Sandy Carnegie Jr. Kevin Cary. Stephen Cefalu. Tripp Cherry. Can Civi. Chip Clark. Meg Clark. Anna Katherine Clemmons. Chris Clunie. Bill Cobb. Hobby Cobb. Winnie Corrigan. Tim Cowie. Mike Craft. Ashley Cramer. Dell Curry. Sonya Curry. Stephen Curry. Chip Davidson. Preston Davis. Seth Davis. Melissa de Castrique Thomson. Mike DeCourcy. Alex Deegan. Ricky Dimon. Scoot Dimon. Heather Dinich. Matt Doherty. Dave Donnelly. Mark Donnelly. Bertis Downs. Gregg Doyel. Chris Dunaway. Chris Dwyer. Greg Dunn. Chris Easterling. Ben Ebong. Alan Edmonds. Dave Fagg. Jennifer Fernandez. Scott Fisher. Bo Fitzgerald. Dave Fleming. Scott Fowler. Jim Fox. Fran Fraschilla. Sterling Freeman.

Ken Garfield. Matt Garfield. Greg Gerdy. John Gerdy. Ward Gibson. Bill Giduz. Mike Giglio. Marc Gignac. Dave Gleim. Wes Goldsberry. Sally Gordon. Jean-Philippe Gosselin. Max Paulhus Gosselin. Conor Grace. Kenny Grant. Brian Grogan. Paula Grogan. Tom Grogan. Chris Gruber. Bill Gullan. Rob Harrington. Steve Hawkins. Henry Heil. Jamie Hendricks. Jeremy Henney. Fred Hetzel. Don Hogan. Terry Holland. Bratton Holmes. Chris Hood. Phil Hopkins. David Houseton. Jason Hult. Rob Hutchinson. Terrell Ivory. Titus Ivory. Jeff Jackson. Reed Jackson. Ian Johnson. Beaux Jones. Kevin Joyce. Andy Katz. Eileen Keeley. Ahad Khan. Meg Kimmel. Landry Kosmalski. Len Kosmalski. Logan Kosmalski. Bro Krift. John Kuykendall. Jim Larranaga. Phil LaTourette. Randy Lawrence. Jack LeFaivre. Ray Logan. Andrew Lovedale. Rick Maese. Phil Martelli. Sterling Martin. David Matheny. Jennifer Matheny. Matt Matheny. Sue McAvoy. Martin McCann. Mark McGuire. Bob McKellar. Kaylie McKellar. Bob McKillop. Brendan McKillop. Cathy McKillop. Kerrin McKillop. Matt McKillop. Sally McMillen. Bridget Meerdink. Jimmy Meerdink. Carolyn Meier. Boris Meno. Susan Mercer. Randy Mitchell. Jody Moore. A.J. Morgan. Jim Murphy. Parks Neisler. Ernie Nestor. Charlie Newton. Eddie Nicholson. Matt Nicholson. Jason Okrzesik. Jon Olin. Jerry Palm. Lucie Paulhus. Cliff Paulsen. Kathy Paulsen. Joe Pearlman. Chris Pearson. Mike Persinger. Damier Pitts. Blake Poole. Joe Posnanski. Jeff Price. Mike Price. Rachel Purcell. Tim Purcell. Terri Peat Purcell. Linda Rae. Joe Reed. Mike Reed. Mandy Rhyne. Jason Richards. Jim Richards. Jip Richards. Lindsay Richards. Mary Beth Richards. Rich Richards. Tom Richards. Austin Rios. Lenn Robbins. Will Roberson. Wendy Roberts. William Robertson. Kevin Rogan. David Rorie. Nancy Rorie. Vanessa Rorie. Tom Ross. Patti Rossiter. Steve

Rossiter. Steven Rossiter. B.J. Rudell. Traci Russ-Wilson. Philip Ruzycki. Jason Sabow. Amie Sander. Jane Sander. Kevin Sander. Thomas Sander. Tom Sander. Lee Sargent. Stacey Schmeidel. Karl Schmidt. Jay Schmitt. Mike Schmitt. Joe Schoenfeld. Scotty Scott. Steve Sechrest. Dick Seidel. Tom Shandley. Steve Shurina. Chip Sigmon. Mario Silva. David Sink. Ashley Smith. Danny Smith. Derek Smith. Adam Soltys. Tom Sorensen. Matt Spear. Adam Stockstill. Steven Suflas. Mike Summey. Lindsay Sween. Tim Sweeney. David Teel. Dave Telep. Pete Thamel. Billy Thom. Rick Thurmond. Jeff Tolly. Ali Ton. Elizabeth Ton. Pierce Trumbo. Rob Ukrop. Bobby Vagt. Jay Wade. Grant Wahl. Doodle Wally. Ben Walton. Mike Weinstein. Langston Wertz Jr. Dan Wetzel. Kyle Whelliston. Jason Whitlock. Allen Williams. Brandon Williams. Brendan Winters. John Woods. Jay Wright. Eric Wruck. Justin Young. Jason Zimmerman.

Also, in 1998, I took off from school what would have been my senior year at Davidson and studied the college's basketball program. My notes from then helped with this project with history and perspective.

Those interviews:

Tommy Abatemarco. Rufus Adair. Chris Alpert. Howard Arbuckle. Rick Barnes. Bill Beermann. Pepper Bego. Jeff Bergmann. Eddie Biedenbach. Taylor Blackwell. Tim Bowker. Michael Bree. Bo Brickels. Bill Briggs. Ken Briggs. Paul Briggs. Bill Brill. David Burns. Tim Caldwell. Danny Carrell. John Carroll. Marshall Case. Steve Clark. Cecil Clifton. Doug Cook. Tom Cook. Tom Couch. Fox DeMoisey. Bob Denham. Scott Denham. Mike Dickens. Lymon Dillon. K.D. Doherty. Mark Donnelly. Chuck Drisell. Lefty Driesell. Paul Drobnitch. Alan Duncan. Bob Dunham. Ben Ebong. Bruce Elder. Dave Fagg. Yates Faison. Ellis "Skip" Finger. Bill Foster. Tom Franz. Edward "Magic" Gaines. Greg

Gerdy. John Gerdy. Maurice "Mo" Gray. Ron Green. George Grimball. Davor Halbauer. Jamie Hall. Ronn Hall. Sam "Pinky" Hatcher. Todd Haynes. Fred Hetzel. J.D. Heuer. Terry Holland. Chadd Holmes. Larry Horowitz. Wayne Huckel. Bobby Hussey. Jim Hyder. Martin Ides. Bill Jarman. Bill Jackson. Dave Johnson. Frank Johnson. Tom Kazee. Steve Kirley. John Kochan. Landry Kosmalski. John Kresse. Bobby Lane. Davis Liles. Jerry Kroll. Rick Lowery. Jim Lowry. Mike Maloy. Charlie Marcon. Stephen Marshall. Sterling Martin. Matt Matheny. Neill McGeachy. Bob McKillop. Bob Moore. Bob Hunter Moore. Luther Moore. Mac Morris. Dave Moser. Jim Murphy. Detlef Musch. Dick Myrick Jr. Janko Narat. Mike O'Neill. Tony Orsbon. Billy Packer. Emil Parker. Chris Pearson. Tom Peddicord. Rick Perkey. Bill Pierce. Matt Pitzer. Max Polley. Jan Postma. Ernie Reigel. Jonathan Rhyne. Pat Riazzi. Jim Richards. Eppa Rixey. John Rogers. Paul Rybiski. Frank Santore. Jay Schmitt. Charlie Scott. Steve Sechrest. Durwood Settles. Steve Shurina. Charlie Slagle. Dick Snyder. Sam Spencer. Ronnie Stone. Lester Strong. J.B. Stroud. Mark Sumwalt. Ed Sutton. Anthony "Ace" Tanner. Barry Teague. Will Terry. Carter Todd. Ali Ton. Cliff Tribus. Brian Turner. Bobby Vagt. Doodle Wally. Gary Walters. Sam Washington. Ed White. Kenny Wilson. Jason Zimmerman.

CBS
WE
BELIEVE
DAVIDSON
WITNE

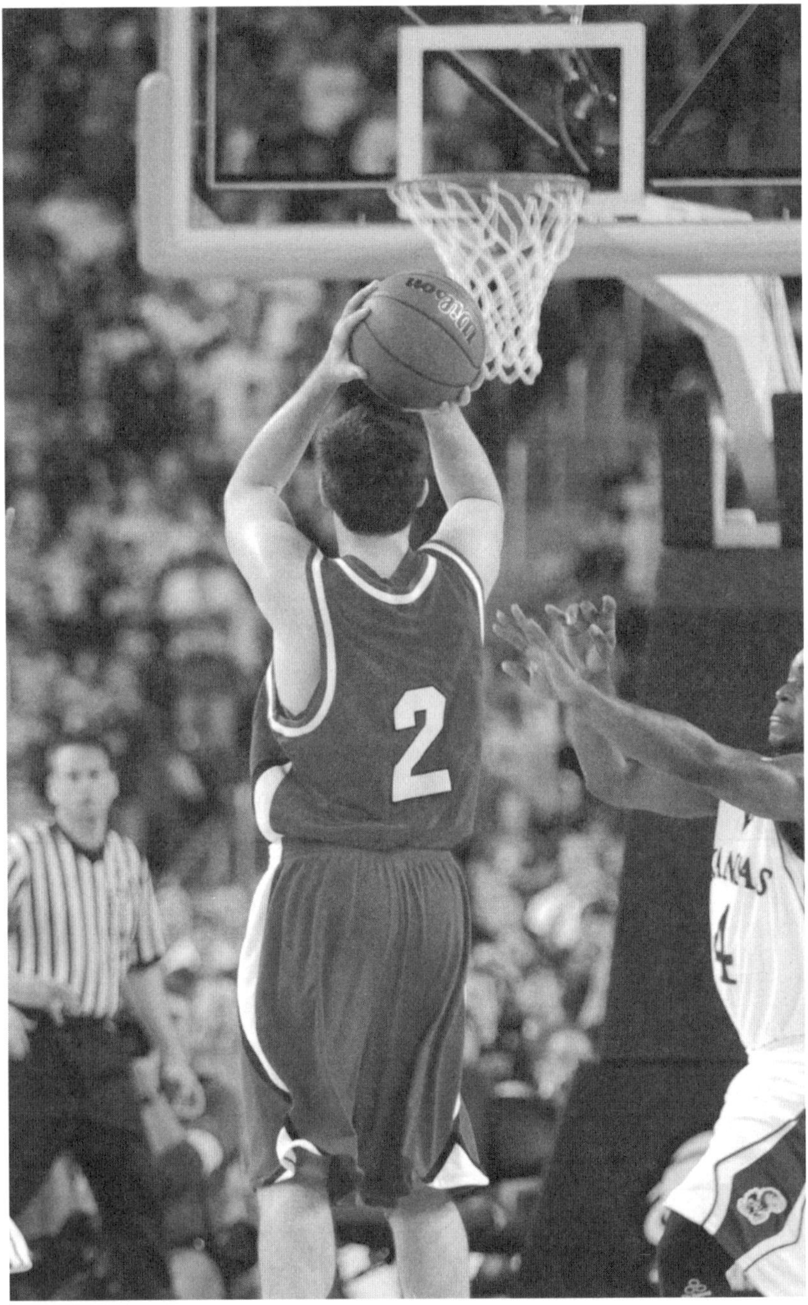

The photograph on the front cover of this book and above was taken by Thad Allender, Director of Photography for the *Lawrence (Kansas) Journal-World.* All other photographs in the book were taken by Tim Cowie, head volleyball coach at Davidson College and a sports photographer who covers a variety of NCAA sports throughout the southeast. Cowie's photographs can be viewed at DigItUpSports.smugmug.com.

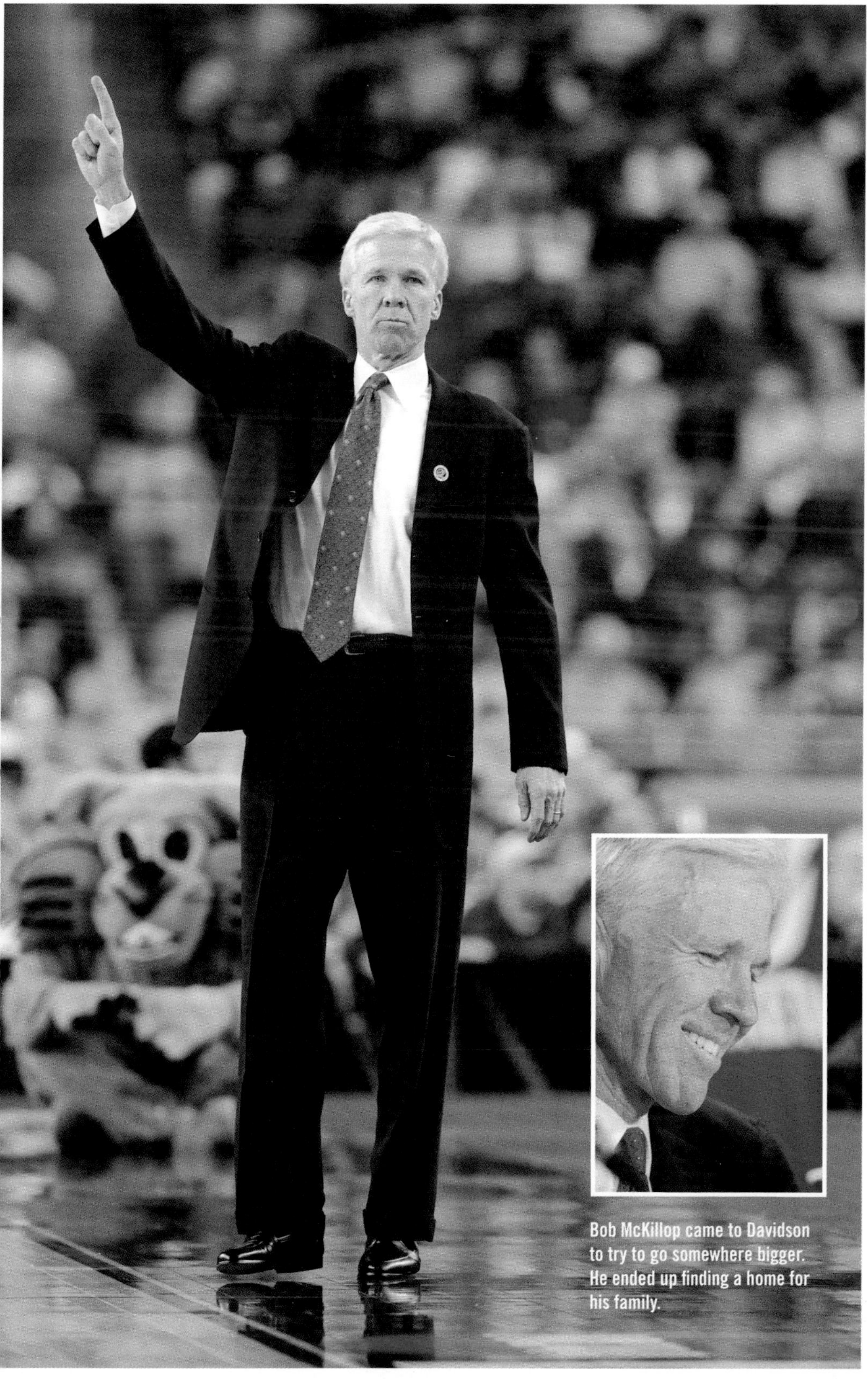

Bob McKillop came to Davidson to try to go somewhere bigger. He ended up finding a home for his family.

Two of Stephen Curry's signature plays of the tournament run: "the scoop" against Georgetown and "the Spiderman" against Wisconsin. It's always the same question. How did he do that?

DAVIDSON
41
WISCONSIN
22

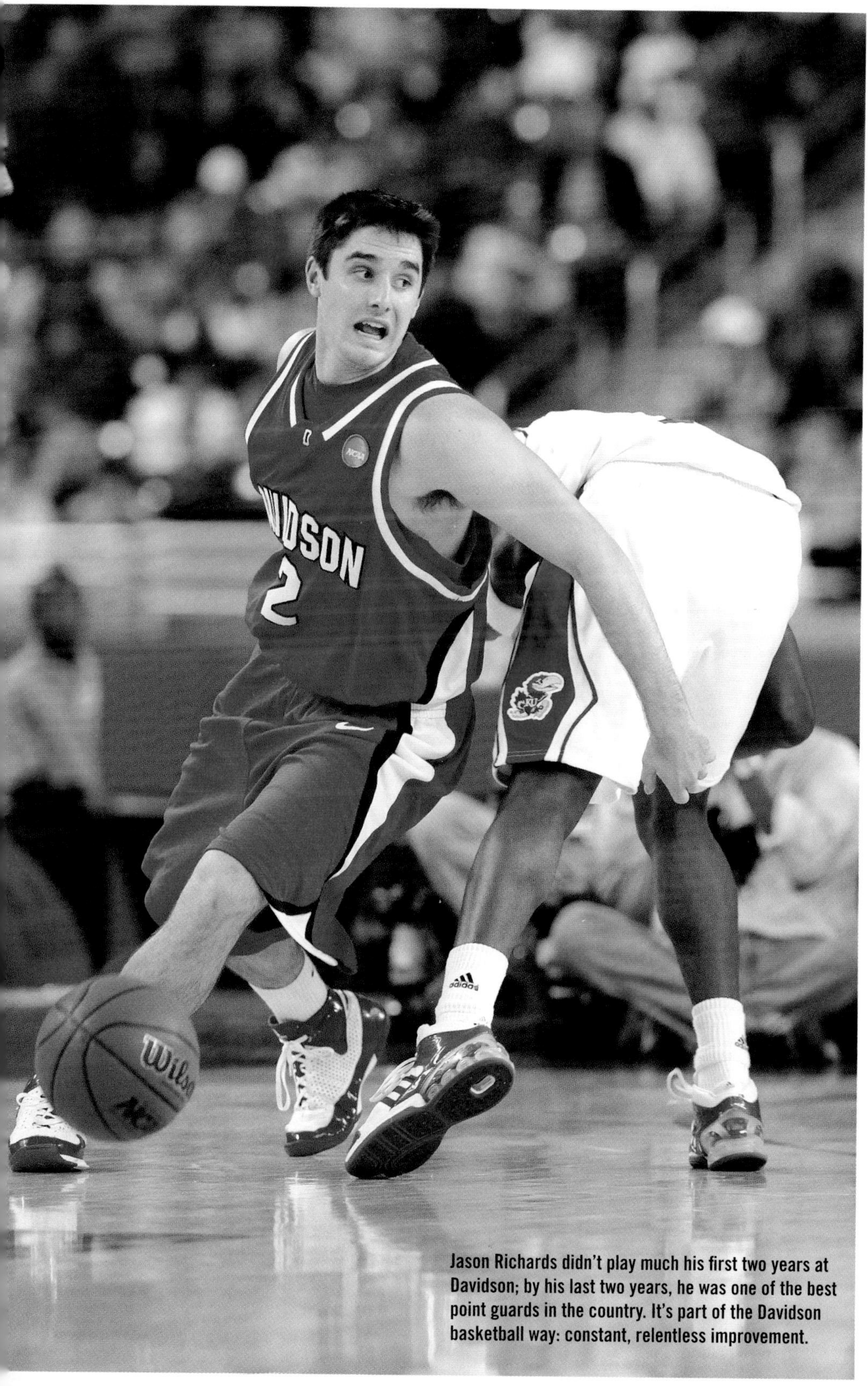

Jason Richards didn't play much his first two years at Davidson; by his last two years, he was one of the best point guards in the country. It's part of the Davidson basketball way: constant, relentless improvement.

Max Paulhus Gosselin playing defense: worth the price of admission.

Bryant Barr: three-point specialist, consummate teammate, math and economics double major — a.k.a. “The White Lobster.”

Andrew Lovedale: one of 10 children from Nigeria, lover and singer of Gospel songs, "a unifying force."

Thomas Sander: “The General,” master screen setter — sometimes down, never out.

Steve Rossiter: "The Colonel," fearless and team-first — here playing Davidson defense. Nothing easy.

Max Paulhus Gosselin and Boris Meno: a French Canadian and a Frenchman, together, on the same team.

DAVIDSON
30

Two iconic images in Davidson: Stephen Curry's No. 30 jersey and the scripture on his sneakers

Some 1,700 students at the school and about 10,000 people in the town — many of them seen here lining the roads in town as the team bus heads to the airport before the second weekend of the tournament.

Don't let your man "go middle." It's one of the main tenets of Davidson's defense. Here, near the end of the Kansas game, Jason Richards, exhausted but determined, strains to keep his man out of the middle — successfully.

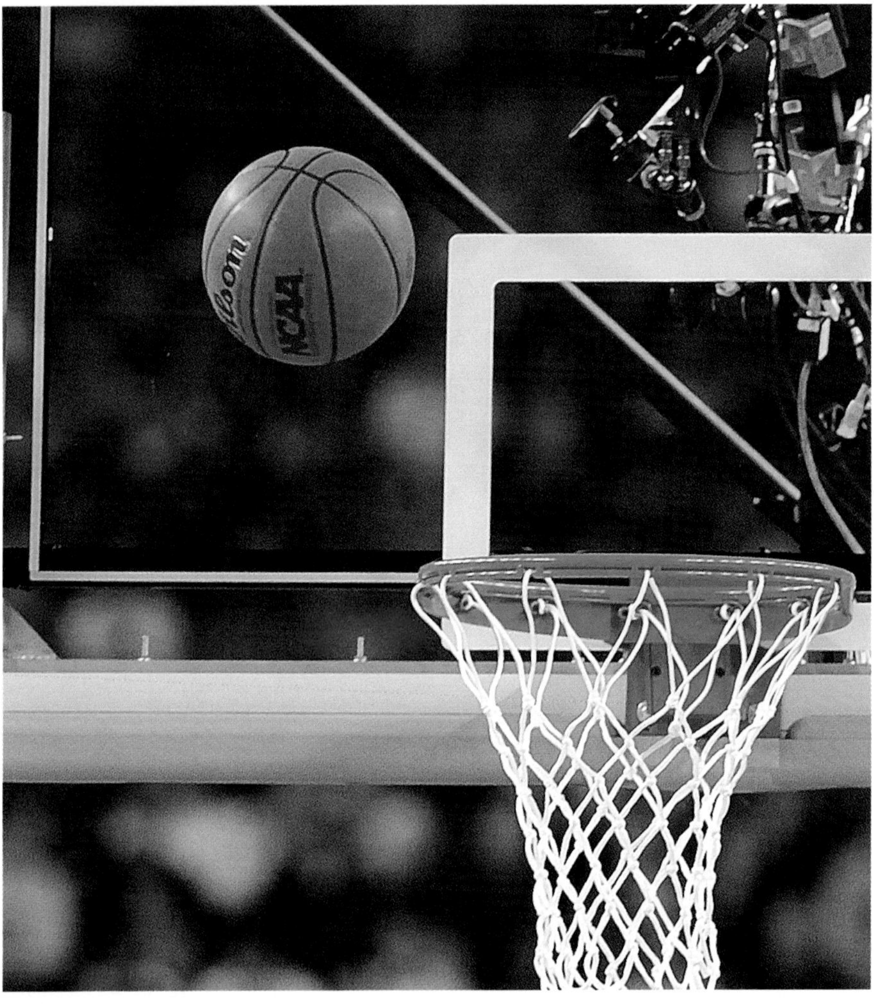

The goal was trust. That goal was not missed.

ADDITIONAL STORIES ABOUT DAVIDSON BASKETBALL

LEFTY, BOB, AND THE KID

Charlotte *magazine, December 2007*

In the beginning there was Lefty. Charles G. Driesell, who went by Lefty and sounded like grits, came to Davidson College in 1960 to coach the basketball team. What he did in the next nine years was, and is, one of the most amazing, most improbable accomplishments in all of college sports – top ten national rankings for the small school, trips to the national quarterfinals, big, loud crowds in the old Charlotte Coliseum. Before the Panthers, before the Hornets and the Bobcats, before UNC-Charlotte was what UNC-Charlotte is today, Lefty's Wildcats were this town's team.

Then Lefty left, in 1969, and went to the University of Maryland, where the pep band played "Hail to the Chief" when he walked into the gym.

Back down in Davidson, the team slipped, first just a little in the early 1970s, then more than that, and by the early 1980s the school's brief, bright blip on the national basketball scene had long since faded to black.

Over those years, and in the years since, Charlotte changed, too. It got bigger, in geography and in population, and with its pro sports teams, its shiny skyline, its creeping reach into the suburbs. Davidson? Even in the mid-1990s, it felt near Charlotte, all the way up in north Mecklenburg County, but it didn't feel like part of Charlotte – too much grass, too much field, too much space, in between, say, exit 18 and exit 30 on Interstate 77.

Now it's almost forty years post-Lefty. Bob McKillop has been Davidson's coach for almost half of those. His team won a school-record twenty-nine games last year, is returning every player of any consequence, is in line for a third straight NCAA tournament appearance, and has on this season's schedule games at Charlotte Bobcats Arena against North Carolina and Duke.

This year could be the year the Wildcats win back Charlotte.

All it took was the legacy of a coach who did his thing and left, the development of a coach who's done his thing and stayed, burgeoning suburbs, and finally a skinny, unafraid nineteen-year-old kid who could end up being the most important player in the history of Davidson basketball.

But wait. That's getting too far ahead. This is, after all, a story about Davidson basketball, and any story about that has to start on the afternoon of April 18, 1960, when athletic director Tom Scott stood up at a Wildcat Club meeting and introduced the school's new basketball coach to the fifteen supporters who cared enough to come.

Lefty Driesell was twenty-eight and balding. He had won a state championship at Newport News High School in Virginia. His first-year contract at Davidson was for $6,000.

"We don't have anything to sell but education," he told the people there that day. "There must be eight or ten good basketball players out there who can get in here. And we're going to find them."

Understand something right now: Davidson does something it shouldn't do when it plays Division I sports. It is a 1,700-student liberal arts school for bookish, serious-minded students, and it has produced doctors, lawyers, pastors, CEOs, and twenty-three Rhodes Scholars. But back in 1960, it was a 900-student, all-male campus, with thrice-weekly chapel and compulsory Sunday evening vespers, a dry campus in a dry county in the middle of nowhere.

The year before Lefty arrived, the basketball team won five games and lost nineteen. None of those wins had come in the Southern Conference. It was, by almost any measure, one of the last places anybody was going to build anything close to a basketball power.

But Lefty was a seller. He sold encyclopedias as a high school coach. He sold the dream of big-time basketball to Davidson prospects and the reality of the education to their mamas. Then he sold Davidson to Charlotte.

He stomped his feet and flailed his arms and slammed doors and kicked volleyball stanchions in locker rooms and called newspaper reporters and talked to them all folksy and nice. He did something that good Presbyterians don't usually do. He evangelized. He sought and got attention.

In his first game as coach, in December 1960, in tiny, brick-walled Johnston Gym, Lefty's Wildcats beat Wake Forest. Billy Packer, now a CBS commentator, played point guard for Wake, and he was so humiliated he went back to Winston-Salem and stayed in his room for the next day and a half.

Before long, the Wildcats were playing in the old Charlotte Coliseum, which is now Cricket Arena, capacity 11,666. There were, at that time, no major pro sports on the East Coast between Washington, D.C., and Atlanta, and the Carolinas' major college teams were in other places, like Raleigh, Durham, Chapel Hill, Winston-Salem, Columbia, and Clemson. The Wildcats' first game in the Coliseum was on December 18, 1962, and the opponent was Duke, and Duke was ranked second in the country, and Duke was the team that lost.

Charlotte had its team. That didn't change for the rest of the decade.

Sports Illustrated ranked Davidson No. 1 in the nation going into the 1964 season. Lefty's teams, in his nine years, beat the teams from Ohio State, Virginia, West Virginia, Alabama, Mississippi State, Pittsburgh, Temple, Memphis, St. John's, Villanova, South Carolina, Maryland, Michigan, and Texas. One team Davidson never beat, though, was North Carolina, and both those losses came in regional finals of the NCAA tournament, by a combined six points, to end the season in 1968 and again in 1969.

Then Lefty left, and that was that. But what happened at Davidson in the 1960s, of course, happened at a different time in a very different Charlotte.

Some dates to consider here:

Man-made Lake Norman was built in 1963.

UNC-Charlotte was created by the state General Assembly in 1965.

Davidson, meanwhile, went coed in 1972.

Interstate 77 from Winston-Salem to Charlotte was finished in 1977. That meant old Highway 21 was no longer the main way to get from Charlotte up to Davidson.

The NBA's Hornets played their first game at the second Charlotte Coliseum in 1988. The NFL's Panthers played their first game in 1995.

Here, then, is the key: All of these dates say something about how Charlotte has changed. The city's population in 1969, when Lefty left, was 240,000. It was 540,000 in 2000, and has gone up by another 100,000 just since then. This isn't just about Charlotte, either, because the transformation of the city made it grow out and up, up I-77, up to the Lake Norman area with all that red-clay shoreline, new roads, new Harris Teeters, new movieplexes, new Starbuckses, fancy roundabouts off Exit 30, hotels, offices, condos to come.

Huntersville, Cornelius, Davidson – they're all doubling in population lickety-split, Huntersville up to 40,000, Cornelius up to 20,000, Davidson up past 10,000. North Mecklenburg High School's student body by now is almost twice the size of Davidson's. The *Charlotte Observer* opened a Lake Norman bureau two years ago. The volunteer fire department in the town of Davidson has had its calls go up more than threefold in just the last ten years.

All that grass between Exits 18 and 30, all those fields, all that space? There's not so much of it anymore. A gap is being bridged.

Enter Bob McKillop. He fits Davidson. Better, truth be told, than Lefty ever did, what with his wire-rim glasses, and his fine suits, and that power dimple tied into his tie. The man won twenty-nine games last year, which is four more than he won in his first three years combined, which at this point seems like a very long time ago.

He is going into his nineteenth season here, and all three of his children have gone here or are going here, and he lives across the street from campus and walks to and from Belk Arena for every game. All of this was never supposed to happen, really, because when he came to Davidson in 1989 from coaching high school at Long Island Lutheran in Brookville, New York, he came mainly to win his way to somewhere else.

Folks forget that. McKillop does not. Quiet bus rides after losses in places like Buies Creek, North Carolina, and Anderson, South Carolina, can humble a man, and did.

"I was brought to my knees," McKillop said one evening this fall out on his back porch.

But his 1993-'94 team went 22-8 and got to the National Invitation Tournament. His 1995-'96 team went 25-5 and undefeated in the Southern Conference. Another NIT.

His 1997-'98 team made it to the NCAAs. His 2001-'02 team got back and lost close to Ohio State. His 2004-'05 team went 16-0 in the Southern and won two games in the NIT. His teams from the last two years: NCAAs again, losses again, close again. Close, close, closer.

Davidson has seventeen basketball alums playing pro ball in Europe. McKillop's teams have grown, and so has he – he delegates more to his staff, he gives more freedom to his players, he's made his playbook more simple. Davidson basketball is a program now.

Last year, something changed. Some sort of tipping point.

Used to be, at basketball games, says Will Bryan, the sports editor of *The Davidsonian*, the school newspaper, "you picked up a ticket, you went and found your friends, you sat with your friends." No big deal. Not anymore.

After last season, the school sent out season ticket information in July, not August or September. "We realized, 'There can't be an off-season this year,'" says Martin McCann, the athletic department's marketing man.

The lower bowl of red seats in Belk Arena is sold out. Just fifteen red seats opened up over the summer, and those people either moved or died. The premium bleacher seats with the backs: sold out. The family pack season tickets: sold out. The ticket office is now selling season tickets in the regular bleachers, which has never happened.

"You go through our database, and there are a lot of Charlotte addresses," says Jamie Hendricks, the director of the ticket office. "We're getting into territory where we've never been before, or not for a long, long time."

ESPN.com ranks the Wildcats No. 24 going into the season. Lindy's preseason magazine has the team at No. 18. *USA Today's Sports Weekly* is predicting a trip to the Sweet 16.

The school has a new athletics Web site, www.davidsonwildcats.com. The arena has a new scoreboard. The media guide is fatter.

Jason Richards is a nominee for the award for the nation's top point guard. Stephen (pronounced STEFF-en) Curry, the star sophomore, is the favorite to win the Southern Conference player of the year. *The Sporting News* is calling him the third-best shooting guard in America. He's one of fifty players nominated for the John R. Wooden Award –

college basketball's Heisman.

Only four schools had their first official practice of this season televised by the ESPNU network. Davidson was one of them.

And one morning earlier this fall, students claimed almost 1,200 tickets for the North Carolina game and the Duke game, both to be played in Charlotte Bobcats Arena. Take away the students who are studying abroad, and there are only about 1,450 students on campus, and many of them spent the night outside the ticket office with beach chairs, blankets, sleeping bags, and tents.

The strangest thing, too, has been happening to Davidson basketball players over the last six or so months. They're getting noticed at the Birkdale Village shopping area in Huntersville and at Northlake Mall in Charlotte. Last spring, Curry and three teammates were on an Easter break road trip, and they stopped at an Arby's somewhere in South Carolina. Five high school kids walked up and wanted to get their picture taken with them.

Then, earlier this fall, someone started a thread on the busy message board at davidsoncats.com. It was titled "Re-Taking Charlotte."

So. Stephen Curry. Last year, the kid who's no more than six-foot-two and no bigger than 190 pounds led the Southern Conference in scoring, dropped 32 points on Michigan in his second college game, 29 in the league championship game, and 30 against Maryland in the NCAAs, and broke the all-time national record for three-pointers made by a freshman. Then he went and made the under-nineteen national team over the summer.

All of this is only the beginning of his potential long-term importance for the Davidson basketball program.

Remember all that space? Stephen Curry can be a sweet-shooting, baby-faced bridger of that gap. Remember all those dates? About Charlotte growing? Here are two more:

On March 14, 1988, Stephen Curry was born in Akron, Ohio, and he was born there because his father, Dell Curry, was playing for the Cleveland Cavaliers.

Three months and nine days later, the NBA had an expansion draft, and one of the two new teams picking that day was the Charlotte Hornets. The Hornets picked Dell Curry. Dell Curry was the very first Hornet.

He was a good player, one of the best shooters in the league, and ended up playing ten of his sixteen seasons in Charlotte. When he retired, he made the city his home, and started the charitable Dell Curry Foundation. He does community relations for the Bobcats. He is part of Charlotte.

So Stephen Curry grew up here. He was an all-state basketball player at Charlotte Christian and graduated as the school's all-time leading scorer. He was small, though, so the big Atlantic Coast Conference schools weren't interested, which is how in the fall of 2005 he committed to Davidson.

Around campus, important people like the athletic director and the new president like to talk about how he's such a good kid, and how he's part of the "fabric," and that's nice.

The Davidson coaches use different words when they talk about him. McKillop: "vision," "balance," "gifted." Matt Matheny, the longtime associate head coach, uses two more:

"Fearless."

"Jugular."

The skinny kid is stronger than he looks. He's cool on the court. He doesn't get riled up and he doesn't get awestruck. He grew up around the NBA. Duke and North Carolina don't scare him.

He also, say the coaches, has some inner assassin. He hunts the big shot, and the big stage, and he has that unteachable something that allows him to miss a shot, two, three...but the next one? It's going in. Last year, in the NCAA tournament game against Maryland, his deep, parabolic three-pointer near the end of the first half went over a seven-foot defender and had Terrapins coach Gary Williams up off the bench cussing and contorting.

"When it's game time, it's game time," Curry said. "I know when to get serious."

He is the kid who can keep the Lake Norman newcomers coming to Belk Arena, and people in Charlotte, too. He is, ultimately, the face of McKillop's rallying cry going into this huge season: "Embrace the bullseye," the coach has said over and over.

What he is, for Davidson, at Davidson, is the son of arguably the most beloved basketball player in the history of the city of Charlotte. What that means, according to Jim Murphy, the athletic director, is this: "Everybody that liked Dell now likes Steph. Which is a lot of people." Which gets back to the premise at the start of this story. Stephen Curry could be the Davidson basketball program's most important player ever.

"It's not out of the question," Murphy said.

"I would say," McKillop said, "he's sort of the post-Lefty poster boy."

Ron Green Sr. was a sports columnist for the *Observer* for a long time. He once wrote this: "If you could capture the magic of the Hornets' early years in Charlotte in a painting, it might be the graceful arc of a Dell Curry jump shot."

That arc now goes up I-77, up to north Meck, up to Exit 30, where this fall little Davidson is heading into its biggest basketball season in nearly forty years. Davidson's reach is moving south, Charlotte's reach is moving north, and this could be the year they meet somewhere in the middle.

Shake hands and say hey there.

How you been?

Long time no see.

LETTER FROM CHARLOTTE

DavidsonCats.com, December 3, 2007

I stood in the back of Mike Krzyzewski's presser Saturday afternoon and listened to him say what he said and thought to myself: I've heard this before.

"They're really good."

Heard it.

"They're an NCAA team."

Heard it.

"They're a very, very good basketball team, coached by one of the best coaches in the country, no doubt about it."

Heard it.

But something I HADN'T heard post-Duke, not working for the *Davidsonian*, not working for the *ACC Basketball Handbook* or ACCToday.com or *Basketball America*, not watching or reading from afar as nothing more than an interested alum, not EVER:

"Davidson could've won."

So Carolina and Duke have come and gone. I would argue Carolina was a coulda SHOULDA. Duke was just a coulda.

From the haphazard notes I was keeping during the game: shotmaking ... Boris miss, miss ... Sander miss ... Sander missed layup ... charge on Steph at 14:00ish ... uh oh ... Lovedale missed runner ... charge at 8:39 Steph ... then Paulus 3 ... Scheyer 2 ... 22-17 ... TO McK at 8:02 ... good TO.

And so on.

Now I see all the predictable gripes about the refs on this board, but the fact of the matter is this, too: Steph scored 20, yes, but also turned the ball over eight times. Jason was great for the most part but also missed six of his eight free throws. Boris missed a dunk.

That halftime score of 43-32 Duke? It was appropriate.

The most striking thing to me about the Carolina and Duke games, and I watched Carolina on TV, and Duke in person, obviously, was that we played … the way we play. We didn't play freakishly, flukishly great, or anything close to it. We just played. We played normal.

And yet No. 1 Carolina needed a pro move from a future pro to finish it.

And No. 7 Duke needed a joke of a shot from Paulus. That THING he threw in on the baseline, he makes that once out of 10 times, maybe twice. It was ridiculous live. It was totally preposterous later that night on the highlights on TV.

But my question for all of you here, and ultimately, I suppose, the point of this post, is, well: IS THIS GOOD ENOUGH?

Let me put it another way:

Still having fun?

I started really thinking about this after talking with Kyle Whelliston at halftime. He said he was there to do another something on Davidson. The two possibilities heading into Saturday's game: (1) Davidson as "conquering hero," to use his term, or (2) "What's the matter with Davidson?"

See the end of Sorensen's column Sunday?

"Here's the best thing about Davidson.

"There was a time when almost beating the Blue Devils and Tar Heels would have excited the team and its fans. That was long ago."

Kinda makes me happy to read that. Also kinda makes me sad.

This IS exciting. This SHOULD BE exciting. We lost by a combined 10 points, on a neutral floor, to two of the best teams in the country. What's the MATTER with Davidson?

Don't get me wrong. I want them to win, get over that hump, whatever. I want McKillop to win one of these games because I think he's an awesome ambassador for my alma mater, and because we're lucky to have him, and because all three of his children decided to go to Davidson, and because I think that's maybe the coolest thing about the man and his relationship with the institution. I want Matheny to win one of these because he went to Davidson, and because he's been at Davidson, and because he's STAYED at Davidson, and because that's worth a lot, because it's stuff like that that makes a place what it is.

But I don't want them to win for me. They owe me nothing.

Maybe that's splitting hairs. I don't know.

One last thing, though: Last Thursday night, I went to a Davidson alumni event in Tampa. Tom Ross was there. These things are always the same, a little cheesy, totally formulaic, but at the same time I'm always glad when I go, because while you're eating shrimp and drinking wine and meeting doctors and lawyers and watching that parade of blue blazers and khakis, you listen to the president give his little status update, about how smart and accomplished this year's freshmen are, and how good Chambers looks now, and somehow it's exactly what I want to hear, because it makes me think about things that make me feel good.

I was born outside Los Angeles. I grew up outside Boston. Since I graduated, seven years ago, I've lived in Charlotte, Chapel Hill, Durham, Wellesley, Mass., Warwick, N.Y., Spring Hill, Fla., Tampa and Land O'Lakes, Fla.

Which, bear with me, is my way of explaining why I got in my car Friday night to drive 569 miles to go see the Wildcats play, win or lose, past the palm trees, away from Florida's loose, sandy soil, up toward all that rich red dirt.

DEAR AMERICA

DavidsonCats.com, March 21, 2008

Dear America,

It was, up until now, a hopeful but hypothetical conversation. We've had it over beers in bars. We've had it on cell phones from Boston to San Francisco, from New York to Atlanta, from Charlotte to Tampa. We've had it in the fall and in the winter, and in the spring and summer, too. We've had it for years.

What if?

What if we won in the tournament?

It's SUCH a good story, we said to each other -- little school, big dreams, cute town, smart kids. People, we kept saying, WANT to tell this story. They just needed a reason. They needed us to win.

This tournament is a series of finite 40-minute windows of opportunity. Seize one and you earn another. Win and you get another two days of news cycle. Win and you get to tell your story.

You have to understand something about us and our school. I don't know if it's Southern gentility or Presbyterian humility, but we've always been institutionally reluctant to say, Hey, look, look at us. It's just not what we've done and so it's not what we do.

But we want so badly for people to know.

So we've looked to Bob McKillop and his basketball team.

He went 4-24 in his first season at Davidson. That was 19 years ago. He has taken us from the Southern Conference tournament to the NIT to the NCAAs and now to a win in the NCAAs. He built this. He didn't leave us when he could have. He has raised his family in a house across the street from campus. His oldest son played for him. His youngest son plays for him now. His daughter went to Davidson and is engaged to a Davidson man. He tears up when he talks about this.

His team went to the NIT in '94.

His team lost in the conference finals in '96 after going undefeated in league play. Another NIT.

In '98, a conference tournament title, a trip to the NCAAs. It seems so, so long ago, but not really, and we were giddy. That felt like this feels. Really it did.

Finally.

There were trips back, in '02, in '06, in '07.

Close, close, close. But never that win.

Now THIS.

Make no mistake: We beat a good team today. This was not about the bounces or the breaks. No. We beat a really good team that played really well because WE played really well.

Because we got a ballsy gutsy late three from Max.

Because we got 13 rebounds from Andrew.

Because we got two huge buckets late from Rossiter.

Because we got nine assists and 15 points from Jason.

And also, of course, because we got 40 from Steph. Not just any 40. An 8-for-10-from-three 40. A 14-for-22 40. A five-steals 40. A first-round-record-setting-40. A forever 40.

But this whole thing is less about how it happened and more about what it means.

After the game, Joey Beeler, the men's basketball media relations guy, was looking frazzled. His life just got crazy. He said his phone started going off right as the buzzer sounded.

Let it be told.

We are one of the smallest schools in Division I.

We are 1,700 students in Davidson, N.C., just north of Charlotte, that's it, all undergrad.

We are NOT Davidson University.

We are ranked ninth in the *U.S. News and World Report* and 23rd in the AP poll.

We keep in touch with our professors after we graduate.

We watch basketball games on grainy Web video from wherever we live.

A couple weeks ago, at the Southern Conference tournament championship game, there was a man with a sign, and the sign said:

YOU

MAKE

US

PROUD

And they do, and in a way that's much, much more intimate than most other Division I program, and certainly most other programs that are playing this weekend for a spot in the Sweet 16. This program, our program, is now big enough to matter but still small enough to touch.

After the game on Friday, in the locker room, there were the lights, the mics, the pens and the pads, the bigness, and there was Steph, surrounded by a scrum three- and four-deep, saying what he said, tired, happy, the faintest of facial hair, as always, on his chin and his upper lip.

We saw in the peach-fuzzed face of this pretty kid from Charlotte the potential of what happened today.

The hypothetical is no longer hypothetical.

He helped make our conversation real.

Sincerely,

Michael Kruse

Davidson College

Class of 2000

WHAT IT MEANS

charlottemagazine.com, March 25, 2008

On the first day of March, in Statesboro, Ga., after the Davidson basketball team beat Georgia Southern to finish the regular season in the Southern Conference at 20-0, I was with Steph Curry with a couple other reporters, and when he was talking to somebody else I happened to look down at his shoes, and what I saw in black Sharpie on the side of one of his Nikes was this: "Romans 8:28."

"And we know that God causes all things to work together for good to those who love God, to those who are called according to His purpose."

Last week, in the NCAA tournament in Raleigh, a photographer captured something similar, in the same neat script, on the side of his shoe.

"I can do all things …"

Philippians 4:13.

So it was that on Good Friday and Easter Sunday, Steph scored against Gonzaga and Georgetown a total of 70 points, 55 of those coming in improbable second-half comebacks on the way to the Sweet 16 – and I'm trying here not to be too, TOO heavy-handed – in which the Wildcats, it could be said, rose from the dead.

Last fall, I wrote a long story for *Charlotte* magazine about this highly anticipated '07-'08 Davidson basketball season, and in that story I posited the theory that this kid, all of 19 at the time, and just turned 20 now, could at the end of his four years be the most important player in the history of Davidson basketball. That idea got stronger and stronger in the course of my reporting. Still, though, I wouldn't have voiced it in public like that if people at the school, in the president's office, in the basketball office and around the athletic department, had at all dismissed the notion when I threw it out there.

Jim Murphy, the athletic director, said it wasn't out of the question.

Bob McKillop, the basketball coach, said Steph had a chance to be a "poster boy" for the program.

Now, sitting here in the Davidson Inn, still trying to process what happened this past weekend in Raleigh, and also what it means and could mean in the future, looking at Steph on the front page of not only the *Charlotte Observer* but the *USA Today*, seeing Wildcat red on the sports front of the *New York Times*, scanning stories online from ESPN.com, SI.com, Yahoo! Sports, CBS SportsLine, the *Washington Post*, the *New York Post*, the *New York Daily News*, *Newsday*, the *Chicago Tribune*, Slate, and on and on and on, I have to say:

We all might have sold the kid short.

He might, in some ways, right now, be the most important PERSON at Davidson, basketball or otherwise, and it took him TWO years, not four.

What he did this past weekend in Raleigh was this: He scored 40 points against Gonzaga. He scored 30 points against Georgetown. He outscored Georgetown's entire team in the last 14 minutes and change on Sunday. He did things to put little Davidson in the Sweet 16 that were unbelievable even to those of us who have been trained to just about expect the unexpected with him.

But what he did, in a broader sense, and what he IS doing, and will continue to do, goes way beyond basketball, and way beyond this week heading into Friday's game against Wisconsin. Here's the thing, and I say this as a Class of 2000 Davidson grad, and also as someone who now makes a living as a reporter at the *St. Petersburg Times*: The small college in the cute, wee town in northern Mecklenburg County, it seems to me, always has had this institutional reticence about being too forward or loud in telling or selling its story, even as the college over the last generation or so has gone from regionally fine to nationally excellent. The thought, rooted, I think, in the school's Southern, Presbyterian makeup, is that braggarts are unbecoming.

It's as if we say, We know what we are, we know what we have. And we leave it at that.

But we want people to know.

We do.

We don't mind answering the questions. What's Davidson? Where's Davidson? But we'd really rather not have to.

And this, I think, is where Steph comes in.

Before I go any deeper, though, I should say that he's not the only guy – he's the star of the show, but he's not a one-man band.

McKillop is the perfect man for his job. He is OF this place, in a way that can come only with time, and an emotional investment and attachment, too, that for him looks like this: His older son played for him. His younger son plays for him. His daughter went to Davidson and is engaged to a Davidson man. He's more than just a coach in this community.

He is 57. Next year is his 20th year here. He's the program's all-time winningest coach and the Southern Conference;s all-time winningest coach. Five NCAAs, three NITs, all those league titles, all those coach of the year awards, all those international pros he's produced. Within this sustained success, and at a really hard place to win in Division I basketball, he's the constant.

I've often thought of the Davidson basketball story as the chase of the chance. The chance to win in the NCAA tournament. The chance to beat the big boys. The chance to match the precedent set by Lefty Driesell way back in the '60s in a very different time. It's the narrative that never ends.

Within that story, though, is the story of a man, and the McKillop story, just over the last few years, I think, has begun to come into sharper focus: He came here to go somewhere else, and says so, and he ended up staying put and finding a home. He lives across the street from campus. He walks to games. His children went to the school he represents. All of this is highly, highly unusual in his mostly greedy, mercenary, job-hopping profession. And it's somehow reassuring for the rest of us who live in this go-go, more-more, what's-next world.

It's instructional and inspirational without being Chicken Soupy or sappy or overwrought.

He's where he's supposed to be.

It's practically a parable.

That sort of continuity and connection seeps into his roster. Take Thomas Sander. He's a senior this year, a captain, but toward the end of his playing career in high school in Cincinnati the thoughtful kid actually was considering not playing in college because he found the recruiting process smarmy and disheartening. McKillop, he thought, was different. Now the econ major is an anchor of a class that has won 100 games – the most of any class in the history of the program – and his trademark might be as a guy who sets screens that are awe-inspiring to those who really know what they're watching when they're watching basketball. Everybody sees Steph's shots go in. Not even close to everybody sees all the things that go into creating those shots.

There's Max Paulhus Gosselin, the selfless, tireless defender from Quebec, a guy whose effort on the court is so palpable I sometimes can't look away.

There's Andrew Lovedale, a testament to the kind of consistent development so many of McKillop's players seem to experience: He started this year as a reserve. He's ending it as a revelation.

There's Stephen Rossiter, the Staten Island son of a New York City firefighter, and I don't mean to gush here, but he's one of the nicest kids you'll ever meet.

There's Jason Richards, the point guard from the suburbs of Chicago, underrated and unflappable, a history major who wrote his thesis earlier this academic year on the African-American reaction to Jackie Robinson and the breaking of the color barrier in Major League Baseball. The first hug he got Sunday night when the bus got back from Raleigh was from Dr. Sally McMillen, his advisor, and also, I should say in the interest of full disclosure, a mentor to me, too, when I was here in school and ever since. Bill Cobb, Class of '84 and one of the Wildcats' most devoted fans, said Monday: "This is our team. It's the community's team. We all won." And I think this is what he means. I don't know Jason the way I knew the guys on the team when I was in school, not by any stretch, but I FEEL like I do, I feel like I know him, and that feeling somehow is because of things like Dr. McMillen giving him that hug. That's something we share.

During my time as a student, I wrote about the basketball team for the *Davidsonian*, and I started a newsletter for fans that still exists, *The Wildcat Report.* After graduating, though, I gradually lost touch, because I had jobs, because I lived for a while up in New York, because then I moved to Florida to work for the *St. Pete Times.*

Last year, though, I was coming through town in December, for the first time in what seemed like years, and to see Dr. McMillen, actually, and I called up associate head coach Matt Matheny and asked if he could get me a ticket for the UNC Charlotte game. He said sure. Left it at will call. This was very early in Steph's freshman season, and I had heard about this special player, this special kid, but I didn't really have any idea. So the Wildcats won the tip, threw it to Steph, and he shot a three, and it missed and came bouncing back to him and he picked up the ball and shot it again and it went in. This was all in, like, the first seven seconds of the game. I might be misremembering. But that's at least the way it plays in my head.

I was captivated as a graduate of Davidson.

I was captivated as a watcher of basketball.

I was captivated as a professional seeker of story.

And it was immediate. Can't really explain. Just was.

So this year I came to Charlotte for the Duke game, I went to Anaheim for the UCLA game, I was in Davidson for weekends when I could get away, I was in Charleston twice, I was in Statesboro. When I wasn't at games – I do, after all, live in Tampa, and have a job that I love and would like to keep – I listened to John Kilgo and Logan Kosmalski on the Internet radio broadcast. I started clicking refresh way too often on the message board at DavidsonCats.com.

Then came Easter weekend in Raleigh.

"There's a lot of joy going through my body," Jason said after Gonzaga.

After Georgetown, McKillop, standing in a hallway under the RBC Center stands, talked about the first moments with his team after the game in the locker room. He talked about joy too. "We just laughed, we just laughed," he said, "because of the joy we felt for each other and our program."

And then there was Steph.

I look at the photo that ran huge on 5C of the *Observer* sports section on Monday, with him running down the court, one finger high into the air, surrounded by the noise of nearly 20,000 strong, and I remember that moment, and I STARE at that photo, at Steph, at OUR Steph, and I look at the one on the front of *USA Today*, the one where he's hugging Thomas, and I look at his face, I STARE at his face, and I can't stop, and I think that's because what I see is absolute, unfettered, childlike joy.

He is the kind of face America loves to love. He was readymade for all of this: the little-guy story, the local-kid-made-good story, the father-son story with his NBA dad Dell. He's accessible, he's approachable, he's attractive. He signs backs of T-shirts, he gets pictures taken with folks' kids, he points up high when he does something good. He praises his teammates for getting him open and finding him shots and he means it.

He was all of this waiting to happen.

Wins over Gonzaga and Georgetown? A spot in the Sweet 16? That wasn't totally predictable.

But the publicity and the attention that's coming from it once this DID happen? That much was.

The other night, after driving from Raleigh to Davidson, I re-read that *Charlotte* magazine story from last fall.

"So," I wrote toward the end of the piece. "Stephen Curry."

Just listen to this stuff now. It's somehow simultaneously prescient and quaint.

"Around campus, important people like the athletic director and the new president like to talk about how he's such a good kid, and how he's part of the 'fabric,' and that's nice.

"The Davidson coaches use different words when they talk about him.

"McKillop: 'vision,' 'balanced,' 'gifted.' Matt Matheny, the longtime associate head coach, uses two more:

"Fearless."

"Jugular."

Then this: "He also, say the coaches, has some inner assassin. He hunts the big shot, and the big stage, and he has that unteachable something that allows him to miss a shot, two, three … but the next one? It's going in. …"

I think of the Georgetown game. Two-for-eight in the first half. Three more misses to start the second. Then 25 of his 30 points in the last 14 minutes and 24 seconds. He can't even explain it.

"He is the kid who can keep the Lake Norman newcomers coming to Belk Arena, and people in Charlotte, too," I wrote last fall. "He is, ultimately, the face of McKillop's rallying cry going into this huge season: 'Embrace the bullseye,' the coach has said over and over.

"What he is, for Davidson, at Davidson, is the son of arguably the most beloved basketball player in the history of the city of Charlotte. What that means, according to Jim Murphy, the athletic director, is this:

'Everybody that liked Dell now likes Steph. Which is a lot of people.' Which gets back to the premise at the start of this story. Stephen Curry could be the Davidson basketball program's most important player ever."

Now, some six months later, here we are.

What Steph has BECOME is the face of the college as a whole.

He is the biggest single reason guys from the Raleigh *News & Observer* and the *New York Post* are writing that Davidson does things the right way and that if they had to do it all over again they would want to come to Davidson. He is the biggest single reason Dick "Hoops" Weiss of the *New York Daily News* was on campus on Monday and couldn't stop talking about this "hidden gem." He is the biggest single reason applications almost certainly will go up, which means the already low acceptance rate almost certainly will go down, which means that already high academic ranking could climb. He is the biggest single reason that thousands of people – millions? – now know what Davidson is and where Davidson is. He is the biggest single reason all those people are starting to know something of what we've known all along. He is the biggest single reason Davidson, with 1,700 students, with an arena with 5,700 seats, in a town of 10,000 people, will play Friday night in Detroit at Ford Field, capacity 72,000.

And he is the biggest single reason I've been back to Davidson more times in the last six months than I had been probably in the previous six years. He is the biggest single reason I have reconnected with people I never should have lost touch with in the first place. He is the biggest single reason I have reconnected with the place I consider my home. And I am not alone.

THIS is what he's doing.

My favorite thing about him, though, is that he doesn't seem to know any of that.

On Monday, I was in the sports information office, and Steph shuffled in, dressed in a hooded sweatshirt and his sock feet, just up from a nap in the team lounge and ready for a radio interview in Toronto. He looked like a sleepy just-turned-20-year-old kid because that's what he was. He rubbed his eyes and cleared his throat and talked to Toronto.

"Everything I've ever dreamed of happening here at Davidson," he said, "it's coming true."

"We have a game coming up against Wisconsin on Friday," he said, "and we believe we can win."

The interview ended, and he got off the phone, and we sat and we talked.

I asked him what he would say about Davidson to all the people out there who are thinking about the school and the team now who were not at this time last week. He thought about that.

"It's a very small place," Steph said, "a unique place, where, I guess – the way we enjoy things all together, with everyone knowing each other, I think the joy is more real. More deep."

He speaks for so many of us.

STAYING STEPHEN

Charlotte *magazine, November 2008*

Not quite 1,700 students are enrolled at Davidson College, and one of them, Wardell Stephen Curry II, is one of the best, most hyped, most visible college basketball players in the country. This is not supposed to happen.

But last March, in the NCAA tournament, Davidson's basketball team won a game, and then another, and then another after that, and fell just two points short of beating eventual national champion Kansas for a spot in the Final Four. CBS took Stephen Curry, son of Charlotte, and made him America's golden boy.

In the spring, he was on Charlie Rose on PBS, The Early Show on CBS, and Late Night with Conan O'Brien on NBC, and he was a finalist for the Wooden Award for the national player of the year. In the summer, he went to the ESPYs as a candidate for breakout athlete of the year, was written about on ESPN.com, on CBSSports.com, on SI.com, and in the *Observer*, and was invited to the elite camps of NBA superstars like Chris Paul and LeBron James.

LeBron's cell?

Kid's got it.

Stephen, pronounced STEFF-in, who won't turn twenty-one until the middle of March, is not the first basketball star at Davidson, and he's not the first basketball All-American there, either. What he is, though, and he is very much this, is Davidson's first basketball star in the televised, talked-about, blogged-about, YouTubed, sports-crazy, Internet-fueled infotainment culture in which we now live. He is a national player of the year candidate, arguably the face of the college game, certainly one of its boldest boldface names. He is a main character in ESPN's spotlit, big-bucks college sports reality-show narrative that never ends. He is also, still, a student at little Davidson College in northern Mecklenburg County.

The Stephen Curry story for two years has been whole heaps of fun. But the truly interesting stuff is just about to begin.

People talk around town. They talk about the team, they talk about coach Bob McKillop, and they talk a lot about Stephen. The talk never really stopped after March, and just kept going through the hot, slow, studentless months, and straight into the new academic year and the approaching start of the new season.

People wonder if Stephen can shift from playing mainly shooting guard to playing more point guard. They wonder if he can play in the NBA. Is he good enough, tall enough, strong enough? "He will play in the NBA," an NBA scout told me last summer. "I see him as a first-round pick in '09." That's if he chooses to leave school early and go pro. Which is another question.

And these are fine questions, all of them, and plenty worthy of fan discussion over coffee at Summit on Main Street, or over beers at the Brick House Tavern in Davidson.

But none of them is the most compelling question.

Can Stephen stay Stephen?

We all have a stake in that.

Before we go there, though, let's talk about how we got here.

It wasn't that long ago, after all, that Stephen Curry was only quasi-known just around Charlotte, and then mostly as the short, scrawny son of former Hornet and overall good guy and community man Dell Curry. At Charlotte Christian, Stephen was 5-foot-6 as a freshman, 5-foot-8 as a sophomore, 5-foot-11 as a junior. His jersey hung on his slender shoulders as if on a wire hanger in the corner of a closet. It wasn't that long ago, either, that he showed up at Davidson for freshman orientation with a microwave, his laptop, four duffel bags, and a red, white, and blue quilt he got from his grandmother as a graduation gift.

Then he went and scored thirty-two points in his second college game.

Against Michigan.

In Ann Arbor.

And it took off from there: Southern Conference freshman of the year, league tournament most valuable player, a college record for three-pointers in a season by a rookie, thirty points against Maryland in the NCAA tournament. Then, last year, his sophomore year, more, more, more: thirty-eight points against Appalachian State, thirty-seven against Chattanooga, forty-one against UNC-Greensboro, league player of the year, league tournament MVP again, second-team Associated Press All-American, and a college record for three-pointers in a season. Not by a rookie, but by anybody, ever. And somewhere in there, somewhere along the way, middle-aged men, Davidson men, serious men with serious jobs, started showing up to games in Belk Arena wearing red No. 30 jerseys.

That took two years.

The whole celebrity thing?

That took ten days.

March 21 to March 30, Gonzaga, Georgetown, Wisconsin, Kansas, and in Davidson's four games in the tournament Stephen scored forty, thirty, thirty-three, and twenty-five points, and none other than LeBron, global basketball royalty, showed up with his posse behind the Davidson bench "to watch the kid," and the rest of the country went bonkers for the guard with the peach-fuzz face.

The AP called him the star of the tournament. So did *USA Today.* So did the *Washington Post.* The *Observer* called him a "national sensation."

The suddenness of such stardom made it intrinsically captivating: Here was one of the best players in all of college basketball, seriously, and before that week and a half most folks didn't even know his name. Davidson people were gleeful, which was to be expected; what was interesting, though, was that everybody else was, too.

Why?

Think about what we cheer for these days. We cheer for home run hitters who turn out to be doped-up frauds. We cheer for star quarterbacks who turn out to be dog killers. Last year, we cheered for the Patriots' pursuit of a perfect 19-0 record, or many of us did, but that pursuit came with an embedded, uncomfortable question: were these guys cheaters? And we cheer for the biggest stars in college basketball every year, even though it's quite clear that most of the highest-tier talents are something other than "real" student-athletes, on campus doing their single, obligatory year before they can play in the NBA, largely unpaid (or at least not legally paid) props who are made to participate in this sham for the purposes of our entertainment and frankly because too many people (who aren't them) make too much money off even their just-passing-through presence.

Maybe that's too cynical. Doesn't make it untrue.

But Stephen?

Sociology major. Lives on campus. Has every year. Lives with Bryant Barr, Steve Rossiter, and Dan Nelms, his teammates and friends. Goes to soccer games. Goes to field hockey games. Goes to frat parties. Celebrity?

Superstar? College kid.

What Stephen became in March was the face of an increasingly elusive guilt-free fan experience.

CBS put the Davidson-Kansas game in pre-*60 Minutes* primetime for a number of reasons, but Stephen was a major factor, the network's senior vice president of programming told me. The decision worked: the ratings for the game were the second-best in that slot in this decade, higher even than the North Carolina-Georgetown game the year before.

Wendell Barnhouse from the paper in Fort Worth, Texas, called Stephen "hypnotic."

"Unlike so much of college basketball," wrote Michael Rosenberg of the *Detroit Free Press*, "Curry is more appealing the closer you get."

"It's impossible," the *Columbus Dispatch*'s Michael Arace wrote, "to take your eyes off him."

Last summer, when I was in Davidson, I went to a handful of late-night pickup games at Belk Arena – current Davidson players, graduated Davidson players who now play pro overseas – and the number of people in the stands, at 10, even 11, was larger on the nights when word had gotten out that the kid was in town.

Plug Stephen Curry into YouTube. Earlier this fall, there were almost 400 videos, some of them homemade highlight reels set to songs with titles like "Superstar" and "Dangerously in Love."

128 points.

160 minutes.

That's how many points Stephen scored in the tournament last year. That's four games on CBS.

That did this.

It's a testament to TV's enormous power. TV takes what it touches and turns it into a commodity. A human commodity is a celebrity. That word makes Stephen hem and haw, but he does cop to this: since last March, his life has changed.

Over the last eight or so months, while working on a book about Davidson basketball, I've spent more time thinking about and talking about Stephen Curry than I probably should admit. I've talked to Stephen, his parents, his high school coaches, his college coaches, his high school teammates, his college teammates, local media folks, national media folks – shoot, I've talked to the kid's freshman-year hall counselors – and so I feel comfortable stating the following: he is in fact what he seems to be.

His apparent humility?

It's not an act.

He's practically bashful.

When he was on Conan, he walked out onto that stage, everybody was clapping, he sat down, crossed his legs, uncrossed them. He seemed jittery. Nervous. People at Davidson noticed it, and loved it. Nobody, not even off to the side, not even in disappointed hush-hush, has suggested to me that Stephen's getting a big head.

It makes some sense when you know that Dell Curry grew up in tiny, rural Grottoes, Virginia, helping his dad, a day-shift machinist for the General Electric factory in nearby Waynesboro, keep the rows of the family's large garden meticulously weedless and straight. Also, this: when Dell Curry came home after his first season in the NBA, he told his dad he wanted to buy him a new pickup truck, and so they went down to the local Chevy lot, and his dad picked out the one he wanted, a nice blue and white one. Used. Stephen might have grown up with the kind of material privilege associated with a father who for sixteen years made NBA money, but he comes just as much from Grottoes, that garden, that pickup. You, son, Sonya Curry often tells her first born, are blue collar.

Barr has lived with Stephen his freshman year, his sophomore year, and lives with him now.

He found out his teammate and good friend was a Wooden Award finalist by reading it on ESPN.com.

"Why didn't you tell me?" he asked.

Shoulder shrug.

Before his freshman season, before any of this, McKillop, the cerebral, silver-haired Davidson coach, told people Stephen was special. He told reporters, told alums, told friends, and he did that because (1) he believed it, and (2) he thought the freshman, eighteen at the time, could handle it.

Now comes this season. It feels different. Expectations are higher than they've been since the late 1960s, when Davidson was a national power, but back then, of course, there was no ESPN.com poll asking America if Davidson can make the Final Four. Heading into this season, for the first time ever, Davidson could be not underrated, but overrated. Stephen is the person most associated with that hype, not because he wants to be, not because his school wants him to be, but because ESPN and CBS want him to be. Because we want him to be.

The people who know Stephen the best say he's ready for all this.

"Remarkably poised," McKillop told me in September. "Remarkably prepared."

But back to the most compelling question.

Can he stay that way?

Can Stephen stay Stephen?

Last spring, in the aftermath of the tournament spotlight, he didn't take the instantaneous hype and turn it into immediate cash by going pro. We find that reassuring. But it also scares us. We wanted him to make the "right" decision. We now want for him to not get punished for it.

Why are we drawn to him?

He scores a lot of points. We like the guys who pass the ball or rebound the ball or dive on the floor, but we love the guys who score, and Stephen has a chance, if he stays for his senior year, to become the NCAA's second-best scorer of all time, behind only Louisiana State legend "Pistol" Pete Maravich.

People say Stephen looks like the water boy, like the kid next door, like the kid who cuts your grass, he looks twelve, he looks fourteen, he looks like he's just been bar mitzvahed. Meg Kimmel, the editor of the *Davidson Journal*, the alumni magazine, puts it like this: "He's still pupating."

How he looks adds to the allure of what he does.

We look at LeBron and say he's strong. We look at Shaq and say he's huge. We look at Kobe and say he's quick. We look at Stephen and say...

How?

Those who know Stephen and know the game talk about how he uses screens, his quick feet, his quick release, his high fatigue threshold, his unusual ability to stop and then start again. Gym jargon. That, or vague discourse on nature and nurture: exposure to the game at a high level at an early age, shot form somehow bequeathed through bloodlines, the notion of some sort of organic, ongoing basketball osmosis thanks to his NBA dad.

When Dell Curry was with the Hornets, and Stephen was a boy, Sonya Curry would sit next to her son at games and ask him: "See your dad?"

Stephen watched those games as a boy in a way that in retrospect was highly unusual. He didn't watch the ball. He watched his dad. What that meant was that he grew up watching the movements of a man who for a decade and a half was one of the world's very best shooters and users of screens. Stephen, of course, didn't think of it that way at the time. He was just a kid who wanted to watch his dad. But still.

When Stephen got to Davidson, the fall of his freshman year, he was bigger, stronger, faster, and taller than he had been at Charlotte Christian. All of that, though, was not what struck the Davidson coaches the most.

Stephen was able to take the information given to him and correct mistakes almost immediately. It wasn't that he never made mistakes. He made a lot of them. He just usually didn't make any of them a second time. McKillop has been coaching for three and a half decades, and he says he has never had a player like that. It was as if Stephen listened to what he was told, painted a picture of the movements in his head, then channeled those movements onto the court, at full speed, the very next play.

ESPN college basketball analyst and Charlottean Jay Bilas said a few months ago on the phone that Stephen is one of the smartest players he's ever seen.

"Not just in college," he said. "Period."

Stephen, he said, has a brain for basketball that is "Einstein quality."

People watching him play don't think about that. They see shots going in. But here's what else they saw last March. Stephen was so attractive, even to strangers to Davidson, because it was clear that he was part of his community. Somehow this came though: what he does and how he does it jive with the ethos of his place.

The former Davidson president John Kuykendall once ran a capital campaign called "A Quiet Resolve." That's Davidson. Kuykendall is an ordained academic who speaks in an avuncular Southern accent, and I met with him one afternoon last summer at the student union.

"I marvel at Stephen Curry," he told me. "He has so much grace in what he does."

Grace?

"There has been, at least to date, and I hope it continues for four years, a kind of innocence, a kind of delight, to what he does," Kuykendall said. "He plays basketball like he's playing pickup baseball in the summertime. There's joy in that act, and that's a mark of grace. His jump shots go in from Cornelius and Huntersville, and he doesn't hang around and say, 'Golly, wasn't I good?'

"I think that's lovely," he said.

Stephen writes scripture on his sneakers. "I can do all things … " Philippians 4:13. Black Sharpie. He has one tattoo. It's new and small and on the inside of his left wrist and reads "TCC" and "30." The letters stand for "trust, commitment, care" – the team motto – and the number is his jersey number. All that is to say: he uses ink differently than a lot of athletes. That's why the interesting words "uncorrupted" and "nonthreatening" come up in conversation about him. But this is not a conversation Stephen wants to have. He does not proselytize, and this, too, fits the institution he represents.

Last March, Kyle Whelliston, who covers mid-major-conference basketball for ESPN.com, wrote on his Web site, midmajority.com, a passage that was particularly keen: "He sees himself as a conduit, not a battery. He doesn't store up God credits for explosive performances later. … He stays grounded because he believes that the divine flows through him, not into him."

Stephen points when he's on the court. He points at his teammates when they pass him the ball and it leads to a score, he points to fans in the stands, he even pointed at his parents after he hit an important three-pointer late in the Gonzaga game in the tournament. What he says with the pointing on the court is something he actually told me on the phone one evening many months later.

"It's not just me."

People saw that in March, they felt that, and not just Davidson people. He was a part of his team, and his team was a part of his school, and his school was a part of the town. He wasn't one-year-and-out on his way to the NBA. He wasn't a mercenary.

There was "of"-ness.

He was a star, and everybody knows a star when they see one, and yet he was very clearly "one of," not "the one." TV picked up on that and went to it like a magnet to metal. TV commodifies by beaming images up and out. But it also quite literally puts a screen between the watcher and the watched. On the Davidson games in March, though, the relationship between the people in the stands and the kid wearing the No. 30 jersey was not one of wanton, arm's-length idolatry. There was not the typical, expected separation.

But here's the twist: what people saw last March that sucked them in – that innocence, that intimacy – is now, ironically and almost inevitably, what might be at risk heading into this season.

Last April, at the postseason celebration at Belk Arena, the college had two men from campus security shadow Stephen.

Over the summer, and into the fall, the basketball office got requests for Stephen's time unprecedented in number and nature.

Can he come to a birthday party?

Can he speak to a church group?

Can he visit an elementary school class?

"The thing we'll have to remind people," school sports information director Marc Gignac told me, "is that he's also a college student."

Will people understand that?

Early one morning this fall I got up to work on this story and in the process of procrastinating I ended up reading a story online from *Details* magazine about Terrelle Pryor and then a story in the *New York Times* on Andy Katzenmoyer. Pryor is a freshman quarterback at Ohio State right now who in high school in Pennsylvania rushed and passed for 4,000 yards and might have been the most recruited athlete in history. Katzenmoyer is the former Ohio State linebacker who was an All-American and was asked for autographs while taking tests but then had two ineffective seasons in the NFL before retiring. Both stories made me think of a recent *Rolling Stone* piece called "The Tragedy of Britney Spears." It contained this insight: "She is intelligent enough to understand what the world wanted of her: that she was created as a virgin to be deflowered before us, for our amusement and titillation. She is not ashamed of her new persona – she wants us to know what we did to her."

I'm not saying the Stephen story is a Pryor or Katzenmoyer situation. And I'm not saying Stephen is going to turn into Britney Spears. I'm definitely not saying that. But all the stories in their own more modern ways conjure some age-old story lines.

Success spoils.

What goes up must come down.

Too much too soon?

We don't know how the Stephen story ends. Not yet. What is known, though, is that Stephen is about as prepared as any twenty-year-old could be to handle what's coming his way. His dad's been there, done that, and he has smart people around him.

So can Stephen stay Stephen?

Maybe the question is more for us.

Will we let him?

Over the summer, talking to hundreds of people about the shot last March that would have put Davidson in the Final Four had it gone in, I heard from more than just a few people an idea that was isolated and self-consciously contrarian, until I kept hearing it – at which point it became fascinating. What these people told me was that in a weird way, and for reasons they couldn't quite figure out, they were kind of glad the shot didn't go in.

The source of the sentiment, I think, has to do with the idea behind that line from the Britney story.

What we did to her.

Last April, at that celebration in Belk Arena where Stephen had the two security guys with him, McKillop stood on the stage and in his speech he referenced the Bible, Micah 6:8.

"Act justly," he said.

"Love tenderly.

"Walk humbly with your God."

The thousands of people at Belk that night clapped and clapped, and then they stopped, and it was silent again, and McKillop said this:

"That's the challenge we now face. We are an elite team. We are on a pedestal. We are on the Broadway stage. … We need you to hold us accountable as we continue to chase our dreams."

Lots of people heard pretty words that night, and I heard them, too. But it's not all I heard. I heard a preemptive strike. McKillop's no rookie. He knows what's coming.

The national media are going to do what they do. In July, Grant Wahl, the college basketball writer for *Sports Illustrated*, came to town. He talked with some of the guys. He met with McKillop. He had beers at the Brickhouse. The story ran in the magazine in September. That was just the beginning.

Stephen is now 6-foot-3 and change. He's not done growing.

Davidson opens the season with the preseason NIT in Oklahoma in November. The team plays Purdue in Indianapolis and West Virginia in Madison Square Garden in December. Duke in Cameron Indoor Stadium in January. Then March.

That's a lot of TV time for Davidson.

Stephen in last year's tournament was an exceptional example of an unexceptional thing: one of the most reliable (and recyclable) characters in our sports culture, the previously unknown March Madness star. Those guys pop up, just about every year, and then they're gone. We chew 'em up. We spit 'em out. Two things are different about Stephen: (1) he wasn't just a one-game or even one-weekend curiosity, and (2) he's still here.

So what now?

What do we do with him?

Davidson doesn't want to promote him at the expense of the team. McKillop preaches team, always has, and his guys believe it. That includes Stephen. The team, after all, finished last season ranked ninth in the nation, which, when you think about it, for a school with 1,700 students, is pretty much absurd. This past July, though, associate head coach Matt Matheny was at a recruiting event in South Carolina, and a woman sitting next to him looked at his shirt – DAVIDSON, it said on the chest – and she looked at him, and said, "Oh, Stephen Curry."

Davidson can't control that.

The school had a full-page ad for season tickets in the *Observer* in September: "30 Reasons to Experience Davidson." Most of the reasons weren't specifically about Stephen. But the biggest image in the ad was of him.

Still, the institutional inclination is to protect him more than promote him, and I think Stephen appreciates that. He sees campus as a haven.

At least most of the time.

In late August a thread popped up on the fan forum at DavidsonCats.com. It was called "Read this – It will make you proud" and was by a poster known as "JerseyLaywer," who in real life is Steven Suflas, class of '73. He's an attorney outside Philadelphia.

"Last Wednesday night," he wrote, "we arrived to move in my youngest daughter as a member of the Class of 2012. As with every year, a group of upper class volunteers were present to help with the actual 'heavy lifting' of freshman gear. After we dropped her stuff outside the basement of Belk, I moved the car to a remote parking area.

"As I was walking back up past Little, I passed the Most Outstanding Player of the NCAA Midwest Regional, heroically trying to carry an incoming freshman's refrigerator up the hill all by himself. I grabbed half of the refrigerator to help and told him how proud he made us all, since at any other school, five kids would be carrying his stuff, instead of him carrying a stranger's stuff. Steph was as humble and polite as you would expect."

I called Stephen to ask him if that's how it happened. He said it was more or less. He said he and Steve Rossiter, his teammate and roommate, had signed up to help on what's known as the orientation team. That's what students on the orientation team do: they cart TVs and dorm fridges and bookshelves into new students' rooms. There were hundreds of students on the orientation team. Stephen was one of them. What he was doing was by definition ordinary.

And yet the reaction on DavidsonCats.com included the following posts.

"We are witness to something very special."

"Amen."

"!!!!!!"

This needs to be said out loud: the only thing that was out of the ordinary about that act was who was doing it. That was the perception. Implicit in that perception is the tacit belief that he is different. Separate. Even if he doesn't want to be. This is when that "of"-ness starts to change, not because of anything he's doing, but because of something we are doing.

Rossiter watched the faces of the freshmen whose cars they approached, and even the faces of the parents of the freshmen, and there often was a moment of surprise, he said, when they realized they were being helped by Stephen Curry. "Like he wasn't human," Rossiter told me. Rossiter saw something important. In a way, for those freshmen and their parents, and unlike most of the rest of the people on campus, he wasn't human.

They had "met" Stephen already, last March, on CBS.

That screen was there.

Not long ago, Stephen told me he had noticed some of the freshmen, at least earlier this fall, taking pictures of him with their cell phones. Weird, he thought. I asked him what he does when those kinds of things happen on campus.

His answer?

He introduces himself.

SOURCES AND NOTES

enrollment of about 1,700 students Enrollment in the fall of 2007 was 1,674.

Davidson is the only school in the *U.S. News & World Report's* top 10 ranked liberal arts colleges that also plays Division I sports. It was No. 9 in the 2008 academic rankings. The other schools in the top 10 were, in order, Williams, Amherst, Swarthmore, Wellesley, Carleton, Middlebury, Pomona, Bowdoin and Haverford. The next-highest ranked college with Division I sports was No. 17 Colgate.

population of not even 10,000 The population of the town at the time of the 2000 Census was 7,139, but that's gone up because of the growth of Charlotte and its suburbs and the area around Lake Norman.

"Cinderella Davidson." March 29, 2008, *New York Post.*

"Cinderella Dances On." March 30, 2008, ABC News.

"Davidson Extends Cinderella Run." Mike Lopresti, March 28, 2008, Gannett News Service.

"stone-cold in love." "Feel good story of the year ends with Self, KU headed to the Final Four," Pat Forde, March 30, 2008, ESPN.com. "Unless you're a fan of Gonzaga, Georgetown, Wisconsin or Kansas, you fell stone-cold in love with Davidson this March. Real scholar-athletes representing a tiny school from a low-profile league. A self-effacing star whose shooting was nothing short of thrilling. A coach who personifies class. Trustees willing to dig into their own pockets to pay for students to come from North Carolina to Detroit to witness this ..."

No. 1 search on Google The Google stats come from Google Trends, distributed March 28, 2008, by prnewswire.com.

mentioned 9,000 times Bill Giduz, May 8, 2008, Davidson. Giduz is the college's director of media relations.

1.2 million hits Stacey Schmeidel, May 8, 2008, Davidson. Schmeidel is the college's director of communications.

record crowd of 57,000 Official attendance was 57,563. That was an all-time record for a regional final.

13.6 million people. Scott Fisher, CBS Sports, June 5, 2008, by phone.

one in five televisions Ibid. And here's Mike Aresco, the senior vice president of programming for CBS, June 5, 2008, by phone, on the decision to put the Davidson game in that primetime slot: "Everything about the Davidson story was made for TV viewership. The only question was: Would you get a competitive game? If it was competitive we knew we'd have a home run. ... Davidson never hit the wall. One of the things that informed the decision was that Duke, UNC, UCLA – they were close games. I didn't think they were going to get blown out. That showed they could play with anybody.

"And Stephen Curry. People wanted to continue to see him play."

The game ended up being the second-highest-rated regional final in the pre-*60 Minutes* slot in the decade. No. 1 was the Kentucky-Michigan State double-overtime game in 2005. The Davidson-Kansas ratings were 19 percent higher than the 2007 game between Georgetown and North Carolina.

"young America at its finest" "All about peace and love," Jay Mariotti, March 31, 2008, *Chicago Sun-Times.* "What I saw was young America at its finest, inches from an all-time sports memory."

"a little slice of what's right." "A little slice of what's right," Jay Price, March 30, 2008, *Staten Island Advance.* "In a perfect world, we'd all grow up in Mayberry and go to college at a place like Davidson, where the honor system is alive and thriving, the students have somebody to fold their laundry so they can concentrate on more important things, and even basketball players do their own homework."

"what's best for the world." "What the world needs now is Davidson," Jason Whitlock, March 30, 2008, *Kansas City Star.*

Here's Whitlock, on May 2, 2008, by phone, on why he wrote that sentence: "Sitting in Bob McKillop's press conference, his message, what he felt like his team represented – I was just very impressed with what he had to say. Listening to him talk, I could tell he had convinced his team that they were part of something bigger than basketball. ... I bought all of that."

What Whitlock wrote in his column the morning after the game was even more interesting and certainly worth thinking about. Here's how it started:

"Davidson stripped me of any pretense. Victory is all that mattered.

"Sunday afternoon, you wanted the Kansas Jayhawks to join the other No. 1 seeds in the Final Four by unleashing a magnificent display of sculpted athletic ability and power. You wanted Bill Self's Jayhawks to look as impressive as Roy Williams' Tar Heels, John Calipari's Tigers and Ben Howland's Bruins.

"Davidson refused to let it happen. For the better part of two hours at Ford Field, the undermanned and better-disciplined Wildcats walked the Jayhawks through a clinic on execution, effort and determination.

"Davidson vs. Goliath was just that, and as the afternoon wore on, you felt a twinge of immorality rooting for the basketball mercenaries instead of the student-athletes. Sure, you wanted Self to exorcise his Final Four demon and KU's seniors to make it to college sports' grandest stage.

"But you would've felt better about it had the top-seeded Jayhawks crushed the 10th-seeded Wildcats and created the impression that a Kansas victory was the only legitimate option. You didn't want to think about it. You didn't want to spend all day with a knot in your stomach and the creepy feeling that Davidson just might be the better team.

"And then, in the final seconds, as Jason Richards unspooled a would-be game-winning three-pointer, you were emotionally down on the same knee as Self, praying that might would trump right.

"Richards' shot banged wide left, preserving Kansas' 59-57 victory and, more embarrassingly, laying bare your win-at-any-cost mentality."

—

The camera shifted Former Davidson assistant coach Jeremy Henney made for me a DVD of the Ford Field arena feed.

walked slowly up the sideline The descriptions of the actions of people in the moment down on the court, here and throughout the narrative, come from the Ford Field arena feed, and also on raw, unedited, mostly unaired footage from the different CBS cameras in Detroit, provided by the network's Mike Aresco, Harold Bryant and Jonathan Segal.

had won more games McKillop finished the 2008 season with 340 wins overall and 194 wins in the league. All Davidson stats, here and throughout the narrative, come from the Davidson sports information office. Thanks to the late Emil Parker, Rick Bender, Joey Beeler, Marc Gignac and their staffs.

meticulous, almost professorial This brief description comes from observation and many interviews.

Some highlights:

Duggar Baucom, VMI head coach, former Davidson assistant, May 6, 2008, by phone: "One of the most organized, meticulous individuals I've ever been around."

Matt Doherty, Southern Methodist head coach, former Davidson assistant, May 8, 2008, by phone: "Besides my mother, he has the neatest handwriting I've ever seen."

Phil Martelli, St. Joseph's head coach, May 8, 2008, by phone: "He has found a place where he can be where it's not a job. He's not working at basketball. He's teaching basketball. Sometimes, at those bigger places, you have to be too many other things. But it's almost like a perfect combination – a school that values teaching, and an extraordinary teacher. I think he's a professor. He's a professor of basketball there."

ultra-competitive Two particularly interesting quotes here:

Brandon Williams, former Davidson player, now Director of Basketball Operations for the NBA, June 2, 2008, New York: "It's a rock and roll world. At some point everybody is lured by whatever it is. It's the bright lights. It's the media. It's the money. It's the women. Or it's the inner desire to prove to people that you're better than they think you are."

Bobby Vagt, former Davidson

president, June 9, 2008, Pittsburgh. What he said: "If Bob McKillop didn't have a giant to slay, he'd have his legs amputated so everybody would be giants."

looked out at his players The nods come from the CBS footage. The thoughts in McKillop's head come from McKillop, May 26, 2008, Davidson.

window unit air conditioner Don Hogan, West Florida head coach, former Davidson assistant, May 20, 2008, by phone.

red shag carpet. Susan Mercer, basketball office secretary, May 8, 2008, Davidson.

folksy, strong-willed That description comes from interviews with many of the men who played for Driesell at Davidson.

mandated attendance at church services *A History of Davidson College*, Mary D. Beaty, 1988.

less than 1,000 men. Ibid.

His first team in its first game Billy Packer was the point guard on that Wake team. "I was so embarrassed as a player," Packer said in 1998, "that I went home and didn't come out of my room for a day and a half."

players who went on to become All-Americans. Fred Hetzel, Dick Snyder and Mike Maloy were the All-Americans Driesell had recruited to Davidson. The night Driesell signed Hetzel, or so goes the story, the coach slept in his white '56 Ford in a filling station near Hetzel's home in northern Virginia. Both men tell that tale. "He was literally living out of the back of his car," Hetzel told me in 1998 in Leesburg, Virginia.

By the time he left On Lefty:

Taylor Blackwell, former Davidson public relations director, November 11, 1998, Davidson: "Lefty did the impossible. He got Davidson to see itself more in the national picture."

Fred Hetzel, May 28, 2008, Leesburg, Virginia: "He believed his own bullshit. But that's what it takes. Lefty had a super ego."

Sam "Pinky" Hatcher, former player, October 1998, Atlanta: "He put Davidson on the map. He made Davidson known to students in the Northeast and Midwest and out West that would have never heard of Davidson. For the fairly modest price of putting up with Lefty, Davidson got fabulous publicity."

Paul Briggs, former player, January 7, 1999, Davidson: "What Lefty does not know how to do, or how to teach, is how to lose, and in life, you find out, there are lots of losses."

Bill Jarman, former player, November 1998, Gastonia, North Carolina. "Lefty used to play players 1-on-1 and he couldn't stand to lose. He'd call fouls if he was in danger of losing."

Jim Hyder, former player and student manager, October 22, 1998, Louisville, Kentucky: "He probably wasn't the kind of guy who would pat you on the back for a job well done as much as he'd chew your ass for making a mistake."

Luther Moore, former student manager, November 1998, Charlotte: "He'd kick stuff. No question about that."

Steve Kirley, former player, January 1999, Clemmons, North Carolina: "He definitely favored the people who were stars. If you were a star, he would kind of overlook things. And if you were winning, anything went."

Davis Liles, former player, November 16, 1998, Charlotte: "Lefty was the best recruiter, and it had nothing to do with basketball. He knew he had one of the best educational institutions in the country. He sold the school before he sold the basketball. If you wanted to be a doctor, a lawyer, a businessman, and were good at basketball, Lefty was your coach. He also had that ability to get along with everybody."

Barry Teague, former player, November 1998, Charlotte: "He always talked to the mamas. My mother loved and adored him."

Dave Moser, former player, November 3, 1998, Charlotte: "That's what I'll give Lefty credit for. He was always psyched up and always had us psyched up and ready to play. Lefty would go into the closet at the Coliseum before games, doing God knows what in there. But when he came out of that closet, he was ready to do battle. What did he do in there? Heaven only knows. By tip-off, we were pretty much in a frenzy."

Charlie Marcon, December 18, 1998, Bethlehem, Pennsylvania: "One of the problems of playing for Lefty was that he'd put a lot of pressure on you for the whole season. The first day of practice was like the final practice of the season. Physically and emotionally, he'd just wear you out; come the middle of February, we were just so worn out."

Bill Pierce, former player, November 18, 1998, Greenville, South Carolina: "He was a character. He walked into a room, and people were drawn to him. He performed. People in the Coliseum came just as much to see Lefty stomp the floor and throw up the left hand."

Jan Postma, former player, December 11, 1998, Spartanburg, South Carolina: "He could talk to you for about five minutes and find out what made you tick, and then he'd sell you on that."

Dick Snyder, former player, November 15, 1998, Paradise Valley, Arizona: "Lefty is not a coach I would want my kid to play for. And yet I've got to give him credit for a lot of things I learned. He taught me how to get through a pick. He taught me footwork defensively. If I had not gone through that I would not have ended up in the NBA. I don't agree with everything he did, but he certainly put me in a position where I had the opportunity to fulfill a dream."

Ellis "Skip" Finger, former student manager, December 18, 1998, Allentown, Pennsylvania: "Like a force of nature."

Cecil Clifton, former player, October 6, 1998, Toccoa, Georgia: "In a sense, he was a little bit of a misfit at Davidson. Even though he graduated from Duke, he didn't come across as an intellectual. But he was smart. Anybody who thinks Lefty didn't know what was going on was ignoring things.

"Lefty's legacy there was an achievement that has been sought since he left."

coming to Davidson "Davidson hires McKillop as cage coach," United Press International, May 20, 1989; "About Face; McKillop learns what it's like to lose," George Usher, *Newsday*, January 20, 1990; "Energy Surge," Chris Hobbs, *Charlotte Observer*, February 25, 1996.

was going to do that again. That comes from McKillop and others. Here's alum and fan Parks Neisler, May 15, 2008, Charlotte: "In the fall of '90, we were walking from Terry Holland's house to the football game, and Bob was dreaming. He said it could be done again."

before all-black Texas Western *And the Walls Came Tumbling Down*, Frank Fitzpatrick, 1999.

Former Davidson coach Bo Brickels, Nov. 16, 1998, Concord, North Carolina: "Lefty Driesell won at Davidson before there was a single black player. Don't ever forget that."

before all-sports, all-the-time ESPN *ESPN: The Uncensored History*, Michael Freeman, 2002.

$6 billion Comes from many sources, including stories about the contract in the *New York Daily News*, the *Dallas Morning News*, the *Detroit Free Press*, the *Los Angeles Times* and the *Chicago Tribune*.

Some perspective on how much things have changed: Driesell made $6,000 his first year at Davidson. Fred Hetzel was an All-American and the first pick of the NBA draft in 1965, and he signed for $20,000.

"I would've taken the Hampden-Sydney job," Driesell told me in 1998, "but they gave it to someone else."

"Today, if you suck, you get $2 million," Hetzel said in 2008. "It's just inconceivable. I can't even relate to it. We never dreamed in a million years that there would be this kind of money in basketball."

five different basketball coaches Terry Holland, 1969-74; Bo Brickels, 1974-76; Dave Pritchett, 1976-78; Eddie Biedenbach, 1978-81; Bobby Hussey, 1981-89.

three more Larry Brown was hired in 1969, Gary Walters was hired in 1976, and John Kresse was hired in 1981. In July 2008, those three were, respectively, the head coach of the NBA's Charlotte Bobcats, the athletic director at Princeton University and the special assistant to the athletic director at the College of Charleston.

Walters, December, 2, 1998, by phone: "When I got down to Davidson, the one group I had never gotten a chance to know was the alumni group. It struck me that the alums had a fundamentally different vision of what they wanted to accomplish. They were under the impression that they could restore the program to the top 10 level. I got the feeling that the alumni expectations were so out of whack with the educational excellence and with how basketball had changed. I was dealing with two mutually exclusive goals, and I felt trapped by that."

Kresse, Jan. 30, 1999, Davidson: "Sometimes you make decisions and find out they're not right and have to admit that. It was very, very hard for me to get past that. It was the most embarrassing time in my entire life."

too many losses Davidson's basketball team had three winning seasons between 1975 and 1989.

Many professors Terry Holland, May 19, 2008, by phone; Sterling Martin, May 19, 2008, by phone.

Retired math professor J.B. Stroud, January 12, 1999, Davidson, on the late '70s to the late '80s: "At that point I did conclude that we were doing the wrong thing by playing Division I."

Tom Kazee, former political science professor, January 13, 1999, Davidson, on Davidson being Division I: "It's like saying you're the most responsible person at the local biker bar. But maybe you shouldn't be hanging out at the local biker bar. … Our profile, in terms of our budget and academic standards, is closer to Division III."

Terry Holland, May 19, 2008, by phone: "Division III was a real option at that time. I felt like we owed ourselves one more chance."

Holland, October 29, 1998, Charlottesville, Virginia: "The niche Davidson has – being the only Division I school in its category – is not something you just throw out the window."

turn down the Davidson job Bob McKillop, June 19, 2008, Davidson. "McKillop Won't Go," Joe Krupinski, *Newsday*, May 3, 1989. McKillop to *Newsday*: "A variety of my needs couldn't be met. Academically it's a great institution. People call it 'the Princeton of the South.' They have an ambitious basketball schedule. It's a great place to raise a family. It was an attractive situation. But we couldn't come to terms on a number of things that were important to me."

accepted a second offer "McKillop Takes Job at Davidson," Mark Herrmann, *Newsday*, May 20, 1989; "College Notebook," *The Sporting News*, May 29, 1989.

"I've been a manager and a decision-maker for years," McKillop said at the sparsely attended news conference to announce his hiring, according to stories in *Newsday* and from the United Press International. "And I'm looking forward to transferring those skills to the college level."

He also said: "I'm accustomed to recruiting kids at Lutheran. It costs $4,500 a year for a kid to go there, and the recruiting is very competitive."

"mustard sandwich sort of guy." Former player Rich Perkey, Oct. 7, 1998, Atlanta: "He was young, energetic and charismatic. He was always saying he was a mustard sandwich kind of guy."

cocky. Jim Richards, alum, April 16, 2008, Davidson: "When Bob came in here, he was cocky as shit." Jay Wade, alum, May 6, 2008, Davidson: "He was as cocky as you could imagine anybody could be. He was going to come down here and turn this program around in no time."

"Are you a dreamer?" Sterling Freeman, May 19, 2008, by phone.

four wins Only one of those four wins came against another Division I team. Davidson beat Central Florida, in Orlando, in front of 417 people. "UCF Can't Extend Streak To 2; Sluggish Knights Deliver Wildcats Elusive Road Victory," Alan Schmadtke, *Orlando Sentinel*, February 25, 1990.

"This is a major adjustment for me," McKillop told *Newsday* in a story on January 20, 1990. "You don't understand what it's like coaching a team that loses until you coach a team that loses."

first team meeting Jay Schmitt, May 21, 2008, by phone: "He looked like one of the most intense people I've ever seen, and he said, 'You're going to be amazed at what you're going to go through.'"

"Run around it" Ibid.

"There were times" Magic Gaines, May 5, 1999, by phone.

"I was in survival mode" Schmitt.

Miami of Ohio A.J. Morgan, May 20, 2008, by phone.

electrical socket Matt Matheny, May 3, 2008, Davidson.

Late in the season Morgan.

the breaking point McKillop, May 13, 2008, Davidson; Jim Richards, April 16, 2008, Davidson; Bill Cobb, April 14, 2008, Davidson; Jason Zimmerman, April 30, 2008, Atlanta. The loss was to Campbell in the Big South conference tournament on March 5, 1992.

Richards: "It was like we were paying respects to the family."

weren't that many fans Lee Sargent, May 16, 2008, Huntersville, North Carolina; Terry Holland, May 19, 2008, by phone.

had come from high school ... Comes from interviews with players on that year's team.

Paul Rybiski, May 9, 1999, by phone: "He went from coaching 15-year-olds to playing Duke, and I think he thought, 'I'm going to go in guns blazing.' It didn't serve him well at all."

Dick Seidel, May 28, 2008, by phone: "We were looking for something to believe in, and we wanted it to be him. But he had a sledgehammer approach."

Rybiski: "For him, it was my way or the highway. He would punch you in the chest. 'You've got to be tough!'"

Seidel: "One time he asked me how I was, and I said, 'I'm okay.' I had some papers and some tests, but he couldn't understand why my response was anything but 'Great!' And he said so."

After the game in Anderson Comes from multiple interviews with McKillop, and also many things he's said about it in different stories over the years.

To Ron Green Jr., *Charlotte Observer*, March 2, 2005: "I thought I could wave a magic wand and move on."

To Mark Herrmann, *Newsday*, Feb. 25, 1996: "I wondered if this was the best move for me. There's a frustration that can cause you to drift."

To Rick Thurmond, *Charlotte* magazine, December 1998: "I really started questioning myself after that third year. The end of that year was probably the lowest point of my coaching career, wondering if I could make it as a Division I head coach."

The point is to share it. McKillop, May 26, 2008, Davidson. "We're all outlets now."

"I came to the conclusion" To Scott Smith, *Charlotte Business Journal*, November 3, 1997: "It took losing – a lot – for Davidson basketball coach to learn how to win. I spent the next month with my family and friends reexamining everything that was part of my life here as a coach. I came to the conclusion that I had done a disservice to my players by thinking only about what winning would do for me rather than giving them an experience they could cherish for the rest of their lives. … I came in here with an arrogance that I could wave a magic wand and take this program to new heights and just move on to another job. To take a job with that kind of focus was absolutely the biggest mistake I could make. It took being brought to my knees, being humbled, having my confidence shaken during those first three years, for me to realize that. … After that miserable night in Anderson, I decided to tell the guys that winning and losing doesn't matter. But if we care about each other, and show we care about each other, winning will take care of itself."

Trust. Commitment. Care. "Davidson has all the markings of a team set to steal the show," Mike Lopresti, *USA Today*, March 24, 2008; "Coach's tenacity drives Davidson," Shannon Ryan, *Chicago Tribune*, March 26, 2008.

"What do you think?" The dialogue in the huddle comes from interviews with the coaches and the players who were in that huddle. That includes: McKillop, May 26, 2008, Davidson; Matheny, May 23, 2008, Davidson; Jeremy Henney, May 7, 2008, Davidson; Tim Sweeney, May 9, 2008, Davidson; Bryant Barr, April 15, 2008, Davidson, and July 9, 2008, Davidson; Max Paulhus Gosselin, April 16, 2008, Davidson, and June 7, 2008, Chambly, Quebec; Jason Richards, April 16, 2008, and June 18, 2008, Davidson; Stephen Curry, April 17, 2008, Davidson, and May 22, 2008, Charlotte; Thomas Sander, April 17, 2008, Davidson; Andrew Lovedale, April 17, 2008, Davidson; Steve Rossiter, May 31, 2008, Staten Island, New York. Not surprisingly, given the magnitude of the moment and the realities of memory, there was not a to-the-word consensus. The words, here and throughout, are true to the sentiment of what was said, if not the exact words.

—

graduates from the 1930s to incoming freshmen John Kuykendall, former Davidson president, May 14, 2008, Davidson.

the college's trustees Tom Ross, current Davidson president, May 27, 2008, Davidson; Wendy Roberts, May 6, 2008, Davidson; Linda Rae, May 6, 2008, Davidson; Traci Russ-Wilson, May 6, 2008, Davidson; Tom Shandley, May 5, 2008, Davidson; Eileen Keeley, June 20, 2008, Davidson. Keeley, via e-mail, August 3, 2008: "Not all did. All *intended* to contribute, but once we hit our number, we stopped reminding them. Almost all did. Plus about another dozen people (at least) who heard about it … responded with a check."

inside Ford Field I was there.

"to watch the kid." "Lebron witnesses Curry carrying little Davidson," Doug Lesmerises, *Cleveland Plain Dealer*, March 29, 2008.

but not quite right Beaux Jones, April 18, 2008, Davidson.

cognitive psychology Karl Schmidt, April 16, 2008, Davidson.

calculus help Zach Calucchia, April 18, 2008, Davidson. He got the help from shooting guard and math whiz Bryant Barr spring semester freshman year. "He saved my butt. He was about like a second tutor for me."

pickup basketball Nathan Bradshaw, April 16, 2008, Davidson. "Kind of the highlight of my whole basketball career."

ate the same food Blake Poole, April 18, 2008, Davidson.

the team's best dancer That comes from Beaux Jones. It's Stephen, by the way. The worst? Thomas Sander evidently is a better screener than he is a dancer.

They saw friends. "Diverse Davidson isn't divided," Vahe Gregorian, *St. Louis Post-Dispatch*, March 23, 2008. Andrew Lovedale: "When I look in the stands, I don't see fans, I see friends."

communal yellow bikes Student James Garrett wrote about them in the Spring 2008 *Davidson Journal*: "A visitor to Davidson may wonder about the bulky, old-fashioned, yellow coaster bikes parked in front of dorms …"

expensive watches Adam Stockstill, May 14, 2008, Huntersville, North Carolina.

lost dollar bills Observed.

YOU MAKE US PROUD That was in Charleston, South Carolina, at the Southern Conference tournament. I was there.

"There they were" Asbury provided print-outs of her journal entries. Here's another entry, from January 20, 2008: "We could have told you that long ago, but we'll jump up and down and let you soak it in for yourselves as you finally figure it out, and as we enjoy the ride that they have every right to take. And yeah, there are ups and downs and profanities and jubilations – but they're always there, and we're always there.

"That's what it is.

"At halftime today, the court was lined with 70 years' worth of men who have left our collective home away from home and made their way out of the bubble to create wonderfully full lives. They came back and stood before us so that we, no longer teenagers but barely adults, could see the significance that this place holds for them, and that there is much more history behind today's dunks and threes and blocks and steals and rap music intervals than we realize. And that our boys, holed away in the locker room planning, have a place in this history – and therefore, so do we.

"It's a humbling feeling. And honestly, it's not humbling because it's basketball and we're oh-so-good at it and we can get national recognition for such a small school; it's because I will always be able to say that I am a part of this COMMUNITY that comes together to support each other, that becomes joyously one in so many ways – because this is only one.

"It feels kind of silly to be so emotional about a basketball team, trying to write about it in such a life-altering sense, and I know that my male family members deserve some of the credit for passing on their intense sports-angst to one of their few daughters. But it's that word up there in caps – the word that inspires so much of what I write, the very real concept that brings a grin to my face at some point every single day – that leads me to this point. Standing there in that arena that only holds about 5500 people, I can scream, jump around, sing, laugh, shriek – I can be completely myself (sometimes with a little extra profanity thrown in) and it's fine with everyone else, it's welcomed by them. I can start cheers if my sports-angsty heart moves me, and people will join in. There I stand in the sold out student section behind the basket, with a very deep knowledge that this is exactly where I am supposed to be – not only in this hour, but in my life. At this place, in the state of North Carolina, in this dorm room writing at 2 in the morning, not knowing so many things. But it's okay, because this place – most importantly, these people – bring me such joy.

"And so it semi-started with a basketball game …"

felt the faces Philip Ruzycki, April 15, 2008, Davidson.

to be a part of something Beaux Jones.

—

Flat The description of the play comes from interviews with many coaches and players. Associate head coach Matt Matheny watched tape of the play with me to help me understand.

Stephen was exhausted. Stephen Curry, March 30, 2008, in the news conference in Detroit after the game: "Their four-guard rotation where they could throw kind of the same defender at you, same style, it really took a toll towards the end."

coach couldn't risk McKillop, May 26, 2008, Davidson.

—

the star of the tournament. Associated Press, March 31, 2008: "star of the tournament." *USA Today*, March 31, 2008: "star of the tournament." *Washington Post*, March 31, 2008: "star of the tournament."

national name. *Charlotte Observer*, March 31, 2008: "national sensation."

He looks like Jerry Palm, collegerpi.com, June 4, 2008, by phone: "He looked like the waterboy. He's going to get carded till he's 40."

Alum John Burns, May 15, 2008, by phone: "He looks like your neighbor's kid, and he just went out there and hit a 30-footer."

Wendell Barnhouse, *Fort Worth Star-Telegram*, May 5, 2008, by phone: "He's fresh-faced. He's normal-sized. He looks like he might break in half."

Alum Stephen Cefalu, May 4, 2008, by phone: "He looks like the middle school kid down the street."

Justin Young, recruiting analyst, rivals.com, April 30, 2008, by phone: "He looks like the kid who cuts your grass."

Joe Posnanski, *Kansas City Star*, May 3, 2008, by phone: "He looks like the little kid that just ran out onto the court."

Landry Kosmalski, former player and assistant coach, May 3, 2008, Davidson: "He looks like he's 12."

Seth Davis, CBS Sports, May 30, 2008, by phone: "He looked like he just got Bar Mitzvahed."

Jason Whitlock, *Kansas City Star*, May 2, 2008, by phone: "He looks intelligent and he looks non-threatening. He looks completely uncorrupted. No tats. He looks like the kid you'd want your daughter to bring home."

Meg Kimmel, *Davidson Journal*, May 7, 2008, Davidson: "He's still pupating."

He doesn't look like Fan Reed Jackson, May 6, 2008, Cornelius, North Carolina: "He looks like he shouldn't be able to do what he can do."

Student Will Bryan, April 14, 2008, Davidson: "He doesn't look like he can do it."

as well as they could have. Gonzaga coach Mark Few, March 21, 2008, in the news conference in Raleigh, North Carolina: "We did everything. We had our man defense where we don't leave him, which we were in primarily. We had a triangle and two. We tried zone, which actually worked very well down the stretch. ... They find him, they know their roles, and you know, we actually guarded him probably, you know, as well as we could."

"all over him." Georgetown coach John Thompson III, March 23, 2008, in the news conference in Raleigh, North Carolina: "He's too good to say you're going to stop him. He has not been stopped all year. No one's stopped him. ... For the most part, he had guys all over him, and the ball was going in."

Stephen was both. Grant Wahl, May 12, 2008, by phone: "Obviously, you had a guy who was the best player in the tournament, and the best story in the tournament. And that's pretty rare." Wahl covers college basketball for *Sports Illustrated*.

"soundbite story" Dan Wetzel, April 30, 2008, by phone: "They could tell his story within five seconds, and you liked him right away. Because everybody's been told no by somebody. ... It's a soap opera. They're just looking for the character." Wetzel is the national columnist for Yahoo! Sports.

People could relate. Alum Adam Soltys, April 30, 2008, by phone: "American males imagine themselves out there on the court, and Stephen allows those people to think, 'This could be me.'" Mike Persinger, the sports editor of the *Charlotte Observer*, May 19, 2008, by phone: "People can see themselves in Stephen Curry."

Stephen had picked Davidson That paragraph comes primarily from Curry and his parents.

As a freshman The heights come from Curry, and also: Shonn Brown, May 15, 2008, Charlotte; Dave Telep, May 14, 2008, by phone. Brown is the head coach at Charlotte Christian. Telep is the national recruiting editor for Scout.com.

"Way overmatched" Eric Bossi, recruiting analyst, May 2, 2008, by phone: "How can you possibly see a Stephen Curry coming?" His evaluation from the NBPA Camp, Richmond, Virginia, June 2005: "Curry, Stephen, 6-0 PG, Charlotte (NC) Christian – Way overmatched from a physical standpoint, but did a solid job running his team. Slender kid who doesn't make mistakes and is smart with his passes and ball handling. Average quickness and shooting ability from deep but always plays hard. Son of Dell Curry. Low major plus/Mid major minus."

look at prospects differently. McKillop, May 13, 2008, Davidson; Matheny, May 3, 2008, Davidson; Jim Fox, May 2, 2008, Davidson; Landry Kosmalski, May 3, 2008, Davidson; Steve Shurina, May 27, 2008, by phone. Kosmalski: "You can see the guys who just aren't competitors."

roughly one in four students who apply. Chris Gruber, Vice President and Dean of Admission and Financial Aid, July 28, 2008, via e-mail. The percentage of applicants admitted was 25.6 for the class that entered in August 2008.

No exceptions. Gruber, June 16, 2008, Davidson: "Our players walk through the front door."

classes with 15 students That's the average. More than 70 percent of classes at the college have fewer than 20 students.

Anderer Peter Anderer, June 2, 2008, New York; Matt Matheny, July 12, 2008, North Augusta, South Carolina.

Bree I was a student when Bree arrived. I was in Chapel Hill the night of the Carolina win.

Pearson Chris Pearson, June 11, 2008, Huntersville, North Carolina.

Another example of this: Davidson once recruited a kid in Denver with no scholarship offers coming out of high school. Brendan Winters graduated in 2006 as the program's all-time fourth-leading scorer. Winters, June 15, 2008, by phone. "Coach McKillop came to watch me in the state semis my senior year in Colorado. That was late March. By then I had no chance for a scholarship." Winters finished with 1,892 points.

McKillop and his assistants Bob McKillop, May 13, 2008, Davidson.

McKillop, March 29, 2008, in a news conference in Detroit: "I saw him play in Las Vegas. He had about nine or 11 turnovers in the first game I saw. I had been recruiting him so I knew how good he was. But I watched the way he responded to the turnover. He got back on defense. He played defense. He didn't try to come down the court and all of a sudden make up for the turnover by taking a crazy shot hoping that by going in people would forget his turnover. He went to the bench and he never hung his head. He patted his teammates on the back. I saw a lot of ingredients that you see today ..."

Matt Matheny, May 3, 2008, Davidson: "He got knocked around off the ball, he wasn't strong enough to battle through contact, he was a little loose with his handle, and he turned it over too much, but he was smooth. And nothing fazed him. ... Almost immediately my first thought was: He's good enough to play for us. My second thought was: Who else is watching? Who else is paying attention?"

Jim Fox, May 2, 2008, Davidson: "He passed it on a line, even though he was, like, 130 pounds."

his senior year Langston Wertz Jr., April 30, 2008, by phone; Jim Fox, May 2, 2008, Davidson; Shonn Brown, May 15, 2008, Charlotte; Randy Mitchell, June 4, 2008, by phone. Also: "Hornets blow lead and then their cool," Seth Emerson, *The State*, December 22, 2005; "Curry, Carter Propel Christian," Langston Wertz Jr., *Charlotte Observer*, January 1, 2006.

Telep The evolution of Dave Telep's Stephen evaluations:

December 2004: "son of Dell Curry; not strong yet but can pass and has feel."

June 2005: "best we've seen him; has hoops IQ; getting bigger; Dell's son can play at this level."

July 2005: "signs point to him making strides; growing, good feel; this guy could wind up being a steal."

December 2005: "leader and stronger; tough kid; shot was slightly erratic; MVP of local tournament."

December 2006: "Davidson/couldn't find his shot in game we saw; needs strength but HUGE upside."

three Davidson coaches Shonn Brown.

surprised everybody but himself. Stephen Curry, April 17, 2008, Davidson; Dell Curry, May 22, 2008, Charlotte; Sonya Curry, June 11, 2008, Charlotte; Matt Matheny, May 3, 2008, Davidson; Bob McKillop, May 13, 2008, Davidson.

"Coach" This interaction comes from Sonya Curry.

"Surprise!" Joey Beeler, former assistant sports information director, May 23, 2008, Davidson; Eric Blancett, May 15, 2008, Charlotte.

word started to trickle Langston

Wertz, *Charlotte Observer*, April 30, 2008, by phone. "People were talking: 'You gotta come see Stephen.' He was blowing up. It was like he was a totally different guy."

That September Fan Danny Smith, June 26, 2008, Davidson. In October, he said something similar at an alumni function in Charlotte: "We've never had a player as special as Stephen."

Telep sent an e-mail The e-mail, provided by Telep, sent November 11, 2006: "I'm going to give you a name that someday I think is going to come into prominence and may be an NBA guy. ... He had a lot of markers and now they are coming to light. He dropped 27 in an exhibition, 15 in the opener and 32 against Michigan on Friday. I LOVED HIM COMING OUT OF HIGH SCHOOL. He was a borderline DI kid as a freshman and when he left as a SR he was the best incoming recruit to the SOCON. Now ... Who knows?" I'm leaving out the name of the team at Telep's request. He has a confidentiality agreement with the team.

By the time he showed up at Davidson Bob McKillop, May 26, 2008, Davidson; Matt Matheny, May 23, 2008, Davidson; Jim Fox, May 2, 2008, Davidson; Tim Sweeney, May 9, 2008, Davidson; Jeremy Henney, May 7, 2008, Davidson. Fox is an assistant coach. Sweeney and Henney were assistants.

McKillop: "He has that ability to transcend the thought process and make an immediate blend of emotional and physical activity. It's almost as though he paints a picture as you speak to him and then follows the path of that picture. ... I've never had a player like him."

Henney: "You could see the other guys thinking. Stephen was just playing."

Sweeney: "As soon as Coach pointed out a mistake, he was able to correct it almost immediately. ... I was a little taken aback."

When Stephen was at Charlotte Christian, before a game in his senior year, Randy Mitchell, an assistant coach, talked in the locker room about an NFL game in which a Patriots player had chased down a Broncos player from one corner on one end of the field to the opposite corner on the other. He drew on a chalkboard in the locker room a diagram of the player's path. The drawing was a triangle. He traced the player's path and asked the boys what that line was called.

They fidgeted.

Stephen spoke up.

"The hypotenuse," he said.

Stephen usually was quiet compared to the other boys on the team, and sometimes that could be misinterpreted as nonchalance. The more Mitchell worked with Stephen, though, the more he knew that was wrong. The kid looked at his coaches. The kid listened.

The kid paid attention.

—

one of the best point guards Wisconsin's Marcus Landry, *Cleveland Plain Dealer*, March 29, 2008: "He was one of the best point guards we ever played."

Coach Bo Ryan, March 28, 2008, in news conference in Detroit: "We said he was the best point guard that we'll face, and he was. It's not always about the points. It's about what he delivers, and he delivers. He can be my mailman."

take the ball where he wanted to take it Ernie Nestor, Elon coach, May 5, 2008, by phone. "Jason took the ball where he wanted to take the ball, and that, simplified, is the definition of good guard play."

when they were *getting* open. Jim Fox.

Pause Davidson game tape Steve Hawkins, Western Michigan coach, May 8, 2008, by phone. "I can remember pausing the film a couple times, and I would pause it as the ball was already out of Richards' hand and before Curry had come off the screen. To me Richards was the player who made them go."

He ran the team. Seth Davis, May 30, 2008, by phone. "There's a difference between running plays and running a team." Davis writes for *Sports Illustrated* and is a studio analyst for CBS Sports.

He picked Davidson over Colgate and Yale. Jason Richards, April 16, 2008, Davidson; Mike Weinstein, May 15, 2008, by phone. Weinstein was Jason's summer basketball coach with the Illinois Rising Stars.

leg cramp Matt McKillop, May 20, 2008, Atlanta; Jason Richards, June 18, 2008, Davidson.

"Crisco" Jason Richards, April 16, 2008, Davidson.

The student managers Mandy Rhyne, May 18, 2008, by phone; Tina Bridgers, May 20, 2008, by phone; Jennifer Fernandez, May 20, 2008, by phone. Rhyne: "I could not believe how hard he was on Jason."

against St. Joseph's "Reserve Is Wildcats' Meal Ticket," Kevin Cary, *Charlotte Observer*, November 27, 2005.

Scared Jason Richards.

"Twelve o'clock rule" Tom Richards, May 16, 2008, Huntersville, North Carolina.

When Jason was a freshman in high school Ibid.

Jason and Lindsay Richards went at each other Lindsay Richards, May 17, 2008, Huntersville, North Carolina; Jason Richards, June 18, 2008, Davidson.

how he had learned to take advantage Tom Richards.

The crowds at away games Tom Richards; Lindsay Richards; Jason Richards; Mary Beth Richards, May 16, 2008, Huntersville, North Carolina.

"I'm right here!" Mary Beth Richards.

The first time Jim Fox; Tom Richards; Mary Beth Richards, May 16, 2008, Huntersville, North Carolina; Tom Allen, May 28, 2008, by phone. Allen is another summer basketball coach who coached Jason.

wanted to win. Jim Fox: "He really, really battled, and he really wanted his team to win."

The coach of the team thought Mike Weinstein: "He took those guys and made them tougher mentality-wise."

hit game-winning buzzer-beaters Jason Richards; Mike Weinstein; Todd Babington, June 4, 2008, by phone; Jason Okrzesik, June 4, 2008, by phone.

"He accepted that role" Todd Babington. In practices, even in the years in which he wasn't playing as much, he had a knack for making shots in drills that mimicked buzzer-beaters. It was uncanny. The coaches used to talk about it.

McKillop sent him an e-mail. Provided by McKillop. From October 15, 2003, to Jason: "There are a significant number of adjustments that every high school player must make as he readies himself to play Division I basketball. Playing defense and being a tough-minded competitor have always presented the greatest challenges in making the transition. Let me first start with tough-minded competitiveness. This is such an elusive talent. It's the ability to play with relentless passion play after play, having the confidence, the emotional toughness to play each play no matter if things are going well or if they're not going well. … Make it a habit by developing the talent every time you step a foot onto the court."

McKillop writes a lot of e-mails to his players. Here's one, provided by McKillop, that he wrote March 7, 2005. His team had just lost in the semifinals of the conference tournament after going undefeated in the league in the regular season.

"Rather than wallowing in pity, I spent the past 48 hours trying to show as much care as I could to as many people as possible. God works in amazing ways. I am motivated, excited, and energized at a very high level right now in preparation for the new season that awaits us.

"I also spent some time 'smelling the roses.' Do you realize that we went unbeaten for 2 months? Do you realize what an accomplishment it is to go unbeaten in conference play? There are 325 Division I teams that play in a conference. We were 1 of 2 teams to go unbeaten. Watching Ohio State beat Illinois yesterday indicates how difficult such a task is. What an amazing story about you guys!

"Did you also happen to see that the top rated team in the RPI, Kansas, lost to Missouri on the same court that we beat Missouri to open the season?

"We have so much to be proud of, so much to be thankful for, so much to be excited about. We need to keep fighting, and keep fighting, and keep fighting."

—

faith Chris Burton, May 2, 2008, Davidson; Beaux Jones, April 18, 2008, Davidson: Claire Asbury, April 18, 2008, Davidson.

Burton: "You had to believe in that moment that anything was possible."

Jones: "There was something about this team. Not one time through the whole tournament did I ever feel like we were going to lose."

Asbury: "This is totally possible."

So close Tripp Cherry, May 26, 2008, Davidson; Bro Krift, June 8, 2008, Pittsburgh.

"Before every game in the tournament" Lindsay Sween, April 18, 2008, Davidson.

in Detroit Nathan Bradshaw, April 16, 2008, Davidson; Chris Dunaway, April 17, 2008, Davidson; Wes Calton, April 17, 2008, Davidson; Jeff Tolly, April 17, 2008, Davidson; Phil LaTourette, April 17, 2008, Davidson; Harper Addison, April 18, 2008, Davidson; Rachel Purcell, April 18, 2008, Davidson; Ashley Cramer, April 18, 2008, Davidson; Joe Reed, May 9, 2008, Davidson; Pierce Trumbo, May 9, 2008, Davidson. Dunaway: "I've gone back and watched it, maybe 10 times or so, just like everybody else, and every time I think: 'We can win this.'"

shoulder-to-shoulder student union Comes from many who were there, including student Mario Silva, April 15, 2008, Davidson; alum Burgin Hardin, May 8, 2008, Davidson; Bill Giduz, May 8, 2008, Davidson.

Brickhouse David Matheny, May 7, 2008, Davidson. Alum Carolyn Meier, May 7, 2008, Davidson.

Providence Road Sundries Alum Ken Garfield, May 7, 2008, Charlotte.

Mercury Bar in Manhattan Alum Jason Hult, May 3, 2008, by phone.

Fox and Hound in downtown Philadelphia Alum Bill Gullan, May 9, 2008, by phone.

the Cheyenne Grill in Atlanta Alum Sue McAvoy organized two evening get-togethers in May with alums who watched the games there in March. The guests included Rob Hutchinson, Tim Purcell, Terri Peat Purcell, Rachel Purcell, Dave Gleim, Ray Logan, Chip Davidson, Charlie Newton, Scoot Dimon, Ricky Dimon, Bob "Butch" Beard, Susan Reid Beard, Clark Candler, Laura Candler and Robert Banta.

to the Lion and the Rose in San Antonio. Alum Chris Dwyer, April 30, 2008, by phone.

Something good was about to happen. Alum Alex Deegan, May 27, 2008, by phone: "I had the same feeling I had at halftime of the Wisconsin game. I felt like something good was going to happen."

"moment of equilibrium." Alum Eddie Nicholson, May 10, 2008, Salisbury, North Carolina.

reawakening of the possibility Alum William Robertson, May 4, 2008, Morganton, North Carolina.

white-haired alum Fan Reed Jackson, May 6, 2008, Cornelius, North Carolina.

almost as if her team couldn't lose Kerrin McKillop, May 13, 2008, Davidson. "I believed we couldn't lose. I really felt like there was some sort of force almost beyond us. It sounds crazy. But I felt like we almost couldn't be touched. I felt like things were just going so right with us. I was convinced we were going to win the national championship."

at home against UNC Greensboro

Student Zach Calucchia, April 18, 2008, Davidson; student Ahad Khan, April 18, 2008, Davidson.

as magical a sequence as he had ever seen. "No Worries, Thanks To Curry," Kevin Cary, *Charlotte Observer*, February 4, 2007.

Back in the spring of 1988 Sonya Curry, June 11, 2008, Charlotte.

"See your dad?" Stephen Curry, April 17, 2008, Davidson.

one of the smartest players Jay Bilas, June 10, 2008, by phone.

saw Stephen do something that was new. Dell Curry, May 22, 2008, Charlotte; Stephen Curry, May 22, 2008, Charlotte.

"It took me five years ..." Dell Curry.

scooped a shot Mike DeCourcy, May 2, 2008, by phone: "It was the most impressive play I saw anybody make in the tournament because he defeated three high-level defenders, all of them bigger than he was, and at a critical moment." DeCourcy covers college basketball for *The Sporting News*.

Stephen *made* it work. Matt Matheny, May 23, 2008, Davidson: "It didn't work great. But it gave him an inch. Which is all he needs."

—

Atchison, Kansas Max Paulhus Gosselin, April 16, 2008, Davidson.

told his parents Jean-Philippe Gosselin, June 7, 2008, Chambly, Quebec; Lucie Paulhus, June 7, 2008, Chambly, Quebec.

doesn't watch sports on television. Max Paulhus Gosselin, June 7, 2008, Chambly, Quebec.

spoke no English Max Paulhus Gosselin, April 16, 2008, Davidson.

majors in sociology Ibid.

where his endless energy comes from Max Paulhus Gosselin, June 7, 2008, Chambly, Quebec.

—

born in Nigeria. Andrew Lovedale, April 17, 2008, Davidson.

sweeping the floor Bob McKillop, May 13, 2008, Davidson. Also, McKillop in a news conference in Detroit, March 29, 2008: "You could just see the genuine care that he had, that he took his job seriously. In order to earn money, he was sweeping the floor in the center. He was coaching young kids in this center. He invested himself in the whole center."

The kids there loved him. John Amaechi, June 10, 2008, by phone.

brings old sneakers Cliff Paulsen, June 13, 2008, Davidson; Kathy Paulsen, June 13, 2008, Davidson.

turned to whip a pass to Stephen The SportsCenter highlights of this pass and Stephen's shot didn't look right if the last part came without the first part. The shot without the pass seemed somehow unnaturally clipped. Will Bryan, a senior at Davidson in 2008, the former sports editor of the *Davidsonian*, pointed that out, and he was right. It was almost impossible to show one without the other. Apropos.

One other note about Andrew: His freshman year at Davidson, at the preseason team tradition called "song fest," where usually the guys howl and razz their teammates for their awful singing, Andrew sang in his deep voice a gospel song called "God Will Make A Way." No more howling and razzing. The room got quiet.

Bryan provided video of that.

"God, I thank you" Andrew Lovedale.

—

roommates Bryant Barr, April 15, 2008, Davidson.

went to church together Stephen Curry, April 17, 2008, Davidson.

be ready for the ball. Bryant Barr, July 9, 2008, Davidson.

son of a retired New York City firefighter Steve Rossiter Sr., May 31, 2008, Staten Island, New York.

special-education teacher. Patti Rossiter, May 31, 2008, Staten Island, New York.

team's only visible tattoo. Steve Rossiter, May 31, 2008, Staten Island, New York.

McKillop went to watch him play Steve Rossiter.

the two of them decided Thomas Sander, July 30, 2008, Cornelius, North Carolina.

considered not even playing Thomas Sander, April 17, 2008, Davidson.

Elder High Mike Price, June 5, 2008, by phone. Price was Thomas' summer basketball coach.

Thomas loved Elder. Jane Sander, May 16, 2008, Huntersville, North Carolina.

didn't trust those coaches Thomas' younger brother started answering the phone when they called.

Thomas?

Sorry.

Not home.

Davidson assistant coach Jim Fox Joe Schoenfeld, June 6, 2008, by phone. Schoenfeld is the coach at Elder.

McKillop was there two weeks later. Ibid.

what he loved Tim Austing, June 6, 2008, by phone. Austing is the assistant coach at Elder.

huddled around him. Bridget Meerdink, May 16, 2008, Huntersville, North Carolina. Meerdink is Thomas' sister.

injuries Ray Beltz, May 13, 2008, Davidson. Beltz is the Davidson team trainer.

take a charge. Thomas Sander, April 17, 2008, Davidson: "There are definitely charges to be taken. People just don't do it anymore. It's a *me* game, it's an *I* game now, and when you take a charge you might get an elbow in the face or a knee in the gut."

The team doctor Ibid.

with a .22-gauge needle Ibid.

Thomas looked away. Thomas Sander.

The locker room Thomas Sander; Brendan McKillop, April 16, 2008; Jason Richards, April 16, 2008, Davidson; Max Paulhus Gosselin, April 16, 2008, Davidson; Stephen Curry, April 17, 2008, Davidson.

"I'll be okay" I saw that in the locker

room in Raleigh.

painkilling shots Ray Beltz.

had to look down at the ball Thomas Sander.

a hand he couldn't even feel. He couldn't feel his thumb and the first two fingers on his right hand.

—

"A changed man" Ben Ebong, June 18, 2008, Davidson.

"Changed completely" Fern Tonella, May 1, 2008, by phone.

more relaxed Ian Johnson, May 5, 2008, by phone: "He was kind of really uptight the first couple years I was there. So intense and so focused. You could sense the aura of electricity. By the time I was a junior and a senior he was much more relaxed. By the time I was a senior I could joke around with him."

more mature as a coach. Chris Alpert, June 2, 2008, New York: "He's mellowed considerably. He's just matured as a coach."

loosened up. Ray Beltz, May 13, 2008, Davidson.

more approachable Eric Blancett, May 15, 2008, Charlotte.

more comfortable Parks Neisler, May 15, 2008, Charlotte: "He's proven himself. I think he's comfortable with who he is."

What's left is confidence. Jay Schmitt, May 21, 2008, by phone: "Now he's calmer, more statesmanlike. He just has that in-control look. There's unbelievable confidence, not that old McKillop cockiness."

lunchtime pickup games Don Hogan, May 20, 2008, by phone. "I remember saying, 'Bob, we're doing this to try to develop goodwill, and I don't think it's working. Some of these professors think we're assholes.'"

rough one-on-one games Jay Wade, April 16, 2008, Davidson, and May 6, 2008, Davidson. "He was in my face, I was in his face – it was a street fight. Bob likes to test you to see how tough you are, and how you're going to take whatever he throws at you, in whatever form it is."

jab his elbow A.J. Morgan, May 20, 2008, by phone; Don Hogan, May 20, 2008, by phone; Bob McKillop, May 26, 2008, Davidson.

Morgan: "The first time he touched the ball he leaned in and threw an elbow at my chest."

Hogan: "I remember the play. Bob was going to test his mettle."

McKillop: "In the world of competition, someone's always going to surrender. When an opponent surrenders, success starts coming my way. The world of competition is all about endurance and surrender. Who's going to surrender?"

jam knives Steve Sechrest, May 23, 2008, Davidson.

tables in hotel ballrooms Ali Ton, May 11, 2008, Roanoke, Virginia.

"put pressure on you" Dick Seidel, May 28, 2008, by phone: "One time he asked me how I was, and I said, 'I'm okay.' I had some papers and some tests, but he couldn't understand why my response was anything but 'Great!' And he said so. … He put pressure on you from the moment he saw you."

a touch of the hand. Martin McCann, May 8, 2008, Davidson. McCann is in charge of Davidson's sports marketing.

the older he gets the more he cries. David Matheny, May 7, 2008, Davidson. McKillop said something along those lines at the April 15, 2008, celebration at Belk Arena: "I find myself crying a lot. By myself."

"I was losing sight of what my mission was." To Chris Hobbs, *Charlotte Observer*, Feb. 25, 1996. "I went through a metamorphosis as a human being because all those things I came to Davidson for had disappeared. Because I was so focused on winning and so focused on being a great coach, I forgot about ministering. I forgot about the players and I forgot about my family. That's a tough thing to think, that you spend 20 hours a day working to be a great program and a great coach and you lose sight of what's really in front of you – your players, your family. Maybe I had to go through that humbling experience and fail as miserably as I did to realize I was losing sight of what my mission was."

"When he became himself" Jason Zimmerman, April 30, 2008, Stone Mountain, Georgia.

1994 Ibid.

handouts Provided by Zimmerman.

Mark Donnelly Mark Donnelly, May 30, 1998, Manasquan, New Jersey; Dave Donnelly, June 8, 2008, by phone.

—

Titus Ivory Terrell Ivory, May 29, 2008, Blairstown, New Jersey; Titus Ivory, June 19, 2008, by phone; "The Wildcats' Inspiration," Peter St. Onge, *Charlotte Observer*, March 28, 2008.

"At the funeral," Terrell Ivory told the Observer, "I was trying to pay attention to everything but what was happening at the front. I remember, vividly, looking up into the back and seeing Coach McKillop walk in.

"Davidson wasn't recruiting me. Coach had no reason to come to my dad's funeral. That's just the kind of person he was.

"I decided that if I was going to spend the next four years of my life somewhere that I was going to go to a place with a man like that."

Another example: In 1999, Phil Hopkins, the coach at Western Carolina, was having problems with his marriage, his son was undergoing tests for cancer, and his team was playing so badly that there were rumors that he was close to getting fired. Western Carolina came to Davidson for a game in January. Davidson won by 37 points. A few days after the game, Hopkins got a letter from McKillop, written in longhand, urging him to keep the faith.

The only reason anybody ended up knowing about the letter happened not quite two months later. In the Southern Conference tournament, Hopkins' team, in a shocking reversal, beat McKillop's team, ending Davidson's season.

Hopkins told reporters after the game about the letter. The reporters asked McKillop if he thought the letter somehow had sparked Hopkins and his team.

"I would do it again," McKillop said.

"If that brought a loss to Davidson College today," he said, "I'd still do it."

"At that time, I was trying to become a born-again Christian, and he knew that," Hopkins told me in June 2008. "He said: 'Don't lose faith.' It was a very personal, very caring letter from one man to another."

Hopkins watched the Kansas game at his home in Tamassee, South Carolina, where he is now a middle school teacher and coach. He prayed for McKillop and his team.

to-the-minute specific McKillop's practice plans are not at all just scribbled on a piece of paper folded up in his pocket. They are typed, they are long, and they are precise. Drills are done in order, and timed, not just in loose increments. Look at a McKillop practice plan and the left side of the pages looks like this:

3:37-3:41

3:41-3:43

3:43-3:45

And so on.

the light in his office Observed.

smile more David Rorie, May 21, 2008, Monroe, North Carolina.

a little more human. Jim Richards, May 17, 2008, Davidson; Bill Cobb, May 17, 2008, Davidson.

started trusting his assistant coaches Steve Shurina, May 27, 2008, by phone; Doodle Wally, May 13, 2008, Davidson.

"hand-across-your-back" Brandon Williams, June 2, 2008, New York. "I think he understands now that you can drive people and hug them at the same time."

Pressure Thomas Sander, April 17, 2008, Davidson.

"We're okay" Brendan Winters, June 15, 2008, by phone.

apologized to them Ali Ton; David Burns, April 17, 2008, Cornelius, North Carolina.

felt at peace. Brendan McKillop, April 16, 2008, Davidson; Boris Meno, April 18, Davidson.

In his news conferences March 29, 2008, in Detroit: "Our system is based on balance. And so few people understand balance. You look at these guys up here. There's a tremendous balance between humility and confidence. Steph Curry has a tremendous balance between fearlessness and patience. And I think our system has a balance between freedom and balance. I think that's something that can be a great example for the world because we need some balance in the world we live in today.

"Parents today abdicate their responsibilities by not disciplining their children and thinking that's love. Love is a balance of that and discipline, in a political world, in the world of the church, in the world of corporations. You could pick your field. There's a complete lack of the balance between love and discipline.

"Parents today, what they want to do is have their children have fun, but yet they don't want to discipline them. They'll let them stay out till 12 o'clock, or they'll let them go to these movies. Sorry, I'm becoming philosophic about this. But that's what's wrong with our world.

"And I think basketball is the world. Basketball is life. And you can replicate on a basketball court what really happens in life. And to see our team, which has the diversity of our team, the cultural, the economic, the religious, the historical diversity of our team to get along as a team, to buy into our system, the world needs to look at that and say, Hey, they can get along together."

March 20, 2008, in Raleigh, North Carolina: "There's a tremendous sense of intimacy that exists between our following and our players. Our players reciprocate in the way we respond to them and our fans, it's a love affair of the heart, not because they have a lot of money and want to be seen. It's a very unique relationship that exists. The cultural diversity of our team, is something I'm so proud of, and maybe it's a lesson for the world to understand that no matter what your color, no matter what your religion, no matter what your nationality, you can all come together for a purpose and the purpose is the team's effort to become the best they can become.

"I have a sense that Davidson is reflecting that in a very small, microcosmic way as a basketball program; and that's not just been this year. That's been a dozen or so years in our program, and that strikes to me as one of the great lessons of college athletics and one of the great lessons of team sports. If you can do it in a competitive, highly-charged atmosphere, why don't you do it in the world?"

"I'm at ease" He said that in a news conference, March 27, 2008, Detroit: "I don't know that I could ever imagine the feeling that this would generate on our campus, in our community, and within me personally."

Rumson Mark Donnelly.

standing and holding his breath. Terrell Ivory.

down the row from him Jason Zimmerman, May 1, 2008, Atlanta.

—

Randy Lawrence Randy Lawrence, May 21, 2008, Davidson, and June 26, 2008, Davidson; Bob McKillop, May 26, 2008, Davidson.

—

"I can do all things ..." Davidson volleyball coach and photographer Tim Cowie took the first shoe photo in March. David T. Foster of the *Charlotte Observer* and Kevin C. Cox of Getty Images took others.

"It's always been one of my favorite Bible verses," Stephen told Kyle Whelliston for ESPN.com on March 29, 2008. "I realize that what I do on the floor isn't a measure of my own strength. Having that keeps me focused on the game, a constant reminder who I'm playing for."

A piece of insight from Whelliston, writing for his own midmajority.com, March 30, 2008: "Getting God on your side in matters of human vs. human competition is complicated, and quite simply impossible. It's also selfish.

"Stephen Curry is the polar opposite of all this. He won't talk about God unless you specifically ask him, and sometimes you have to knock a few times before he'll answer. His shoe quote, Phillipians 4:13, in its full form, is one of the most simple, brilliant and beautiful statements of faith ever written, and it can be easily retrofit to fit any belief system there is.

"Why is Curry so calm in the face of all this pressure, all these tens of thousands? Because he sees himself as a conduit, not a battery. He doesn't store up God Credits for explosive performances later. ... He stays grounded because he believes that the divine flows through him, not into him."

Romans 8:28 I saw that in Statesboro, Georgia, after the last game of the regular season.

the way Dell Curry used to point at his father Dell Curry, June 29, 2008, Charlotte.

family wealth. Andrew Lovedale, April 17, 2008, Davidson. "You don't care if your brother is richer than you. It's family wealth."

noticed the gesture Matt Matheny, July 12, 2008, North Augusta, South Carolina.

SportSouth Marc Gignac, May 23, 2008, Davidson; Joey Beeler, May 23, 2008, Davidson.

No secret Comes from the news conference March 29, 2008, Detroit.

—

four McDonald's All-Americans. Mario Chalmers in 2005; Darrell Arthur and Sherron Collins in 2006; Cole Aldrich in 2007.

four players who were 6-foot-9 or taller. Darrell Arthur is 6-9, Matt Kleinmann is 6-10, Sasha Kaun and Cole Aldrich are 6-11.

five players who in three months would be drafted In the June 2008 draft, Brandon Rush and Darrell Arthur were drafted in the first round, and Mario Chalmers, Darnell Jackson and Sasha Kaun were drafted in the second.

won more games Kansas is behind only Kentucky and North Carolina.

altar boy Bob McKillop, June 19, 2008, Davidson.

small row house with a low concrete stoop. Observed, 11525 122nd Street, May 31, 2008, Queens, New York.

fourth-shortest boy Bob McKillop, June 19, 2008, Davidson.

same green coat and black tie "Energy Surge," Chris Hobbs, *Charlotte Observer*, February 25, 1996. "At Chaminade High, an all-boys Catholic school, the dress code was sports jacket and tie. Other kids wore different ones every day; McKillop wore the same – an Army-fatigue green jacket and black tie."

church bingo Ibid.

He was cut Bob McKillop, May 13, 2008, Davidson. "Sunday night, you know the cut list is going to be posted Monday morning, you get off the bus, you put your hand on the sheet, your heart's pounding, your hands are shaking ..."

more than just about anybody in his neighborhood Kevin Joyce, June 10, 2008, by phone. "I grew up in Bayside, Queens, and I moved out to North Merrick in the fifth grade. He was the only guy in my neighborhood who played basketball as much as I did." More Joyce on McKillop: "He knew the game. He was a good passer. He was very competitive. We were the best two-on-two team around."

made varsity Bob McKillop, May 13, 2008, Davidson.

started only one game *Charlotte Observer*, February 25, 1996.

East Carolina and Hofstra Bob McKillop, June 19, 2008, Davidson.

team MVP in 1972 "Perseverance Has Its Rewards," Mark Herrmann, *Newsday*, February 25, 1996.

NBA tryout Bob McKillop.

players who remind him of *him* Brendan Winters, June 15, 2008, by phone.

paint-stirring sticks Jay Wright, July 1, 2008, by phone. Wright, the coach at Villanova, had his team in Detroit, too. Villanova lost to Kansas in the Sweet 16. The day before that game, though, Wright saw McKillop in the hallway, and he showed him notes he had saved from the lecture McKillop gave in 1984 at a summer camp at Long Island Lutheran High School. "He was stunned," Wright said. Wright also mentioned a McKillop term from those lectures a quarter-century ago. "A tuxedo player," Wright said. "A guy that looks cool. As opposed to a guy who plays hard and doesn't care what he looks like."

One five This comes from a team handout from years ago titled "What is Davidson Basketball?"

"Our five guys" Max Paulhus Gosselin, April 16, 2008, Davidson.

Davidson basketball over McKillop's 19 years I've been watching McKillop's teams play, some years more than others, since 1995, when I was a freshman at Davidson covering the team for the *Davidsonian*, the student newspaper. But to really even begin to understand the "system," if that word's okay, the X's and O's and some of the philosophy behind them, I got lots of help from current and former coaches and current and former players over the spring and summer of 2008. That group includes, in no particular order, Mike Schmitt, Will Archambault, Bryant Barr, Jason Richards, Max Paulhus Gosselin, Stephen Curry, Andrew Lovedale, Thomas Sander, Boris Meno, Aaron Bond, Jason Zimmerman, Matt McKillop, Bob McKillop, Brendan McKillop, Fern Tonella, Jim Fox, Will Roberson, Matt Matheny, Can Civi, Chris Pearson, Ben Ebong, Steve Rossiter, Brandon Williams, Peter Anderer, Terrell Ivory, Billy Armstrong, Chris Clunie,

Brendan Winters, Conor Grace, Ian Johnson, Kenny Grant, Steve Shurina, Ali Ton, Eric Blancett, Logan Kosmalski, Landry Kosmalski.

Little things "What is Davidson basketball?" From the handout:

"You will be taught details, tricks of the trade, insights, and Little Things that are very simple but when added up together they result in producing big things.

"You will rehearse the Little Things over and over until they become habits.

"You will master these Little Things and they will be done instinctively at each opportunity that is presented.

"You are intelligent enough to commit yourselves to use these Little Things to give us an edge.

No fear of physical contact. "You have to hit flesh," Stephen Curry said in a news conference, March 28, 2008, Detroit.

Finish. It's the seventh of McKillop's seven keys: Act. See. Talk. Flesh. Balance. Details. Finish.

"Attack the attacker" McKillop was asked a question in the news conference after the Kansas game. It was the second-to-last question. It started: "Can you talk about the game plan going into this game against a well-known athletic team … ?"

McKillop's answer, some 10 minutes after a two-point loss in a regional final against one of the best college basketball programs in history, with its cadence and its metaphors, to me says so much about the man and his philosophy, and seems as good an explanation of Davidson basketball as there's ever been.

"Attack the attacker," McKillop said. "We will not back down from anybody. We see ourselves sometimes in the middle of the boxing ring and we always want to fight stepping forward and we always want to be in the middle. We understand we're going to get knocked to the mat. We understand we may get knocked to the ropes. But we also understand that we may have to fight it outside the ring, and get into the street, and maybe even go house to house, and we're going to do that."

When we win Comes from the handout: "What is Davidson basketball?"

Defense Bryant Barr: "The way we play defense, it's not you versus your man; it's your whole team against their whole team." Boris Meno: "It just seems like to play good defense now you need shot blockers, athletes who are very intimidating – that's who people talk about. For us, you need to beat not one guy – you need to beat five guys. … If you beat Max, I'm going to be there; if you beat me, Thomas is going to be there."

no easy dribbles Max Paulhus Gosselin: "I want every second to be bothered."

middle Matt Matheny, July 13, 2008, North Augusta, South Carolina. Jason Richards: "The basket is the president, the ball is the bullet, and all five defenders are the Secret Service."

"opposite of any stereotype" Rick Barnes, July 12, 2008, by phone.

"good kids who are fighters" Matt Doherty, May 8, 2008, by phone. Doherty is now the coach at SMU.

Fran Fraschilla, May 7, 2008, by phone: "I would call it an elegant toughness." Fraschilla is an ESPN college basketball analyst.

Duggar Baucom, May 6, 2008, by phone: "You think about the Big East being physical or the Big 10 being physical. But there's a difference between being *big* and being *physical*." Baucom is a former Davidson assistant coach who is now the head coach at Virginia Military Institute.

turning those weaknesses into strengths A flawless player isn't going to come to Davidson to play basketball. Davidson gets players in some ways *because* of their flaws.

Too small.

Too slow.

On defense, for instance, many Davidson players aren't as fast as their opponents from Duke or North Carolina, or even Chattanooga or Georgia Southern in their own league. But they know that, and they also know that if they can't move their feet as fast as the other guy, what they can do is put them in the right places, and at the right times – and they must. There is no choice.

military-style Brandon Williams, June 2, 2008, New York.

"Sometimes you don't learn lessons from winning." McKillop to Tommy Bowman, *Winston-Salem Journal*, March 19, 2008: "Sometimes you learn lessons from losing. You get knocked to the mat, but great people get up. It's how you respond that defines who you are and your character. And we got knocked to the mat, with no embarrassment."

time to do that One summer Boris Meno stayed in Davidson to work on his game and try to gain weight. He wanted to play more, and wanted that right away.

McKillop came up to him one afternoon.

"Boris," he said, "how do you eat an elephant?"

Boris was confused.

"An elephant?" he said.

"Yes. How do you eat an elephant?"

"I don't know."

"One bite at a time," McKillop told him.

Also, all year long, the team kept a jar in its locker room in Davidson, and in that jar were pennies coaches gave the players after practices. A penny per player per practice. In the beginning of the season the jar was almost empty. At the end it was just about full.

two juniors and a sophomore Brandon Rush and Mario Chalmers were juniors. Darrell Arthur was a sophomore.

step-skipping Jay Bilas, June 10, 2008, by phone: "Davidson had seniors, time together and a superstar. I don't think there's parity in college basketball. I think that's a fallacy. The mid-majors are the same. The majors are what's different. They have kids coming and going. I think the majors are more susceptible. We live in a culture of skipping steps now."

finished well The '91 team won three of its last four games, the '92 team won four of its last five, and the '93 team did the same thing.

"did not surrender" "'Businesslike' Davidson Plays On," *Washington Post*, March 28, 2008. "Whether we have gotten to the Sweet 16 or won 28 games," McKillop told the *Post's* Camille Powell, "we have won because we have this belief that's been lived."

—

Months later William Robertson, May 4, 2008, Morganton, North Carolina; June 4, 2008, Davidson; June 14, 2008, Davidson. Robertson: "The moment of brokenness can be the moment of enlightenment. The moment of confusion can be the moment of enlightenment. We are attracted to the stories that contain both the light and the dark."

Romans 5 That's a paraphrase, and there are different versions, obviously, but here's the King James scripture: "We glory in tribulations also: knowing that tribulation worketh patience; and patience, experience; and experience, hope: and hope maketh not ashamed."

"I trust your Garden was willing to die..." www.emilydickinson.it/l0661-0690.html.

—

Cate Bell Cate Bell, May 10, 2008, by phone.

Jennifer Matheny Jennifer Matheny, May 27, 2008, Davidson.

Tripp Cherry Tripp Cherry, May 26, 2008, Davidson.

—

summer of 1989 Bob McKillop, May 13, 2008, Davidson; Cathy McKillop, May 23, 2008, Davidson; Kerrin McKillop, May 13, 2008, Davidson; Matt McKillop, April 30, 2008, Stone Mountain, Georgia.

Kerrin and Matt didn't want to go. Interesting: In the summer of 1962, when Bob McKillop was 12, his family moved from Queens to Long Island. He didn't want to go. He ripped the For Sale sign from the ground in front of the family's row house and threw it in the trash.

"Many tears" Cathy McKillop.

"Because we're different" Kerrin McKillop.

McKillop could have left Davidson in 1994. "Hofstra, McKillop Might Be Good Fit," Steve Marcus and J.P. Pelzman, *Newsday*, February 22, 1994: "Davidson coach Bob McKillop, the former coach of Long Island Lutheran High School, is considered by some sources to be the frontrunner."

pulled his name "Hofstra search widens," *Newsday*, March 26, 1994; "Hofstra to Name Wright Head Coach," J.P. Pelzman, *Newsday*, April 14, 1994.

He could have left in 1998. "Red Storm Starts Search For Coach," Judy Battista, *Newsday*, May 20, 1998; "Storm Coach List Down to 4," Darren Everson, *New York Daily News*, May 20, 1998; "St. John's Talks to McKillop," Jim Utter, *Charlotte Observer*, May 22, 1998;

"Manetta's Not Tipping His Hand," Lenn Robbins, *New York Post,* May 28, 1998; "Storm Eyes Davidson's McKillop," Judy Battista, *Newsday,* May 29, 1998.

interviewed twice Bob McKillop, June 19, 2008, Davidson.

hired Mike Jarvis "Jarvis Talks to St. John's," Mark Asher, *Washington Post,* June 2, 1998; "Jarvis Puts SJU On Hold; Storm's Offer May Not Be Enough For GW Coach," Lenn Robbins, *New York Post,* June 3, 1998; At St. John's, a New Era Requires a Big Name," William C. Rhoden, *New York Times,* June 10, 1998; "For 'Unbelievable Opportunity,' Jarvis Heads to St. John's, C. Jemal Horton, *Washington Post,* June 12, 1998.

He could have left in 1999. "McKillop A Must For Stony Brook," Steve Marcus, *Newsday,* May 12, 1999; "McKillop to stay at Davidson after weighing Stony Brook job," Associated Press, May 22, 1999; "McKillop Jilts Stony Brook, Remains Coach at Davidson," Jeff Williams, Paul Moran, Steve Marcus, *Newsday,* May 23, 1999.

a close friend "McKillop Being Courted; Stony Brook Has Ties to Davidson's Coach," Rick Bonnell, *Charlotte Observer,* May 14, 1999.

six-figure offer "With McKillop Saying No, Stony Brook Needs Pecora," Steve Marcus, *Newsday,* May 26, 1999. "I was secure for the rest of my life with the offer," McKillop told *Newsday* on March 25, 2008.

When it came time for Kerrin to pick a college Kerrin McKillop; Cathy McKillop; Bob McKillop.

Matt's decision Matt McKillop; Bob McKillop; Matt Matheny.

He called other coaches McKillop talked to John Beilein, Phil Martelli, Jim Larranaga and Billy Hahn.

asked Matt to ride the team bus Matt McKillop, May 1, 2008, Atlanta.

"Do you know what this means?" Ibid.

Matt McKillop had been a ball boy growing up. He went to Davidson basketball camps as the chubby little coach's kid. He went on road trips. He watched film with the team for fun. He went to Charlotte Catholic High School and had a decent career there and then went for a year to prep school in New Jersey to try to earn a Division I scholarship. Colgate wanted him. Davidson's coaches thought he could play for them. What if, his prep school coach asked him, his dad wasn't the coach at Davidson? Would he still want to go there?

Matt told him he couldn't think about it that way.

His dad *was* why he wanted to go.

Matt wasn't that fast. He wasn't that tall. He had achy tendonitis in his knees. But he could shoot, and he could think, and he could try so hard because he cared so much. He was like his dad: He was emotional, in a fiery, rah-rah way, but he also wasn't afraid to cry. And he was the only player on the team – perhaps the first player in the program's history – who had grown up rooting for Davidson. One longtime fan started calling him "the program incarnate."

brought his friends home with him for dinners Will Roberson, May 2, 2008, Charlotte; Kerrin McKillop, May 13, 2008, Davidson; Eric Blancett, May 15, 2008, Charlotte; Logan Kosmalski, May 17, 2008, Davidson; Kenny Grant, June 8, 2008, by phone; Brendan Winters, June 15, 2008, by phone; Chris Clunie, June 15, 2008, by phone; Conor Grace, June 17, 2008, Davidson; Ian Johnson, June 17, 2008, Davidson. Roberson: "Matt would just come over for dinner because that was his house, and he would bring Ian and Brendan with him – whereas before it was more scheduled, more structured."

a liaison Matt Berman, June 14, 2008, by phone: "I think Matt helped facilitate a dialogue that maybe other classes didn't have."

asked so much of his own son Chris Clunie: "Matt didn't want to disappoint his dad, and his dad didn't want to disappoint Matt, and I think that permeated throughout the team."

like his sons "Coach Pushes Wildcats to Win," Al Myatt, Raleigh *News & Observer*, February 7, 2004. "Matt has made me a better coach. He's kind of like a string around my finger because I want to treat all my players like they're my sons."

McKillop in a news conference, March 20, 2008, Raleigh, North Carolina: "If you want to be a successful coach, you have to understand that your players are somebody's son. I have often asked about coaching my son, and now I have my second one playing for us, and it's a constant reminder to me that every guy on my team is somebody's son. And I think when you have that understanding in your relationship with your players, it fosters, it embraces a sense of love and care between player and coach ..."

one of the great gifts Cathy McKillop.

Here's a gift:

McKillop once talked about a game in January of Matt's freshman year. The game was at Virginia Military Institute. Davidson was down by a point. Two seconds to go. He called a timeout to plan a last shot, and he felt himself not wanting to draw a play that could lead to Matt taking the shot. He wanted to protect his son from the misery of maybe missing. He was a father first. But this was an epiphany for McKillop: All of his players had fathers, or mothers, or families, and he knew that before, but he hadn't *felt* it like this, ever. So he drew up the play. Matt was not the first option. But the ball got to him anyway, and he took the three-pointer from the right corner ...

And he missed.

It wasn't *like* family anymore.

It *was* family.

white handkerchief Jason Sabow, May 8, 2008, Davidson; Meg Clark, May 8, 2008, Cornelius, North Carolina; Chip Clark, May 8, 2008, Cornelius, North Carolina.

—

Rudell B.J. Rudell, May 18, 2008, by phone.

hit pause At this moment, when

Rudell's TV was paused in Washington, D.C., Davidson sophomore Wes Calton was up in the stands in Detroit, feeling the way he had felt right before he proposed to his girlfriend over Christmas break. Everything had led to this moment. The ring was in his pocket. All he had to do was reach down and pull it out. All he had to do was ask.

Say yes, he thought to himself in Detroit.

Those were the words running through his head.

Say yes.

Say yes.

Say yes.

Down closer to the court, Ashley Smith, Class of 2002, felt the way she had felt at Myers Park Presbyterian Church on May 8, 2004, after the bridesmaids had gone away, when it was just her and her father, and the music changed, and the wedding director opened the doors, and all that was left was to be surrounded by people she loved and to walk from the vestibule into the sanctuary, and down the aisle, and up to the altar.

—

"can magically create opportunities" Bob McKillop, May 26, 2008, Davidson.

decided he had to move Jason Richards, June 18, 2008, Davidson.

—

Watching this now in the student union Sally McMillen, May 2, 2008, Davidson.

"The player and his mother." "Memories Remain For Bradley And Carr," Connor Ennis, *New York Times,* March 28, 2008.

clipped the story Mary Beth Richards.

once had asked Jason Sally McMillen.

—

In Washington B.J. Rudell, May 18, 2008, by phone.

good friend Chris Hood, June 5, 2008, by phone.

thanked them Rudell.

the e-mail Provided by Rudell. Here's the full text of the e-mail, sent December 19, 2002:

"Coach McKillop:

"I just want to express my appreciation for all of your efforts toward fielding competitive basketball teams during your tenure. I remember hearing discussion (though stifled) among the administration several years ago that Davidson might have to consider moving to Division III. It broke my heart.

"But your repeated recruiting and retention successes have made Davidson a more nationally recognized basketball program, which, in a small way, makes an alumnus like me extremely proud. In a larger way, your efforts hopefully have helped quell any doubts that Davidson can triumph both academically and athletically.

"So thank you for your dedication to excellence. And know that you and your team have many fans who live too far away to come to the games, but no doubt cheer just as loudly as those who do."

McKillop had written back Provided by Rudell.

"The face of this NCAA tournament." "Davidson whips Wisconsin," Mike Jensen, *Philadelphia Inquirer*, March 29, 2008. "As long as they last, they are the face of this NCAA tournament."

"The Wizard of Oz in short pants." Mike Lopresti, Gannett News Service, March 29, 2008: "Magic? No, it's Davidson. This is no longer reality. This is the Wizard of Oz in short pants. Davidson 73, Wisconsin 56."

"... story of the year in college basketball." Pat Forde, ESPN.com, March 30, 2008: "This was the feel-good story of the year in college basketball. Maybe of the decade – no disrespect to George Mason. Maybe several decades."

"... a message for the world." Jason Whitlock, *Kansas City Star*, March 30, 2008: "What the world needs now is Davidson. Kansas is taking on more than just a basketball team riding a hot-shooting guard and a winning streak. The Jayhawks are taking on a coach and a team that believe they have a message for the world. Yeah, it sounds crazy, but it's also dangerous. McKillop has captured the minds of his players. He has them believing in a bigger cause."

—

at the student union Mario Silva, April 15, 2008, Davidson; Lindsay Sween, April 18, 2008; Sally McMillen, May 2, 2008, Davidson; Bill Giduz, May 8, 2008, Davidson; Stacey Schmeidel, May 8, 2008, Davidson; Burgin Hardin, May 8, 2008, Davidson.

—

locker room Tim Cowie, May 6, 2008, Davidson; Tom Sorensen, May 19, 2008, by phone. Also helpful were the images in the photo galleries from the *Charlotte Observer*, the *Kansas City Star* and the *Lawrence Journal World.*

—

"We were in the lobby" Lindsay Richards, May 17, 2008, Huntersville, North Carolina.

—

New York Peter Anderer, June 2, 2008, New York.

—

Two days later William Robertson, May 4, 2008, Morganton, North Carolina.

"I've seen some pictures of Stephen Curry" The full text of Robertson's post: "I've seen some pictures of Stephen Curry since Sunday, and he has been smiling. I haven't seen any pictures of Jason Richards, but I hope he's smiling also. Because the last play of that great game was a very good play. It was probably the perfect play.

"Jason had a good, clear shot, and Stephen did exactly the right thing to get the ball to him. I don't know as much about basketball as many people here, but I know that all this was just fine. It was in perfect harmony with this team's way of doing business, a way that got them to the regional finals. Some people who are new to all this may not know exactly what it means to play in the regional finals, but that game is, in my observation, the heart of the tournament.

"I don't have the numbers in front of me, but I'm guessing Jason was somewhere in the 30 to 40 per cent range on three pointers in the tournament. The shot he took was a little beyond the line, so let's say it was a 30 per cent shot.

"Three times out of ten, it goes in. Seven times it doesn't. Let's talk first about the seven. That's where Coach's emphasis on Trust comes into play. I can't take that shot, because I don't have the strength of character to take what happens if I miss. But Jason took the shot, because he had the nerve to do it, and I suspect, because he Trusted the coach and his teammates to continue to love him if he missed the shot. And maybe he had some sense that all the Davidson people, even all the general public, would also continue to love him if he missed. Subsequent events have proven that trust to be well-founded, and that is probably why all this is worth the amount of attention we have given it.

"Now let's consider the three times the shot does go in. It is instantly the greatest moment in college basketball history. Christian Laettner's shot would be the equal in some ways, but essentially allowed a team to win a game it was reasonably expected to win. To do the same thing as such a clear underdog, to get a team to the FF for the first time, would be exponentially more dramatic.

"The very fact that such a turn of events would have been so dramatic, so joyful for so many people, makes the sense of loss all the more painful, and consequently puts even more emphasis on the value of what Jason did in taking the place of Teddy Roosevelt's man in the arena who 'fails while daring greatly; so that his place shall never be with those cold and timid souls who know neither victory nor defeat.' If I could meet Mr. Richards, I would simply shake his hand and thank him for doing this thing while wearing the name of our school on his jersey.

"As a Southerner, I cannot help thinking about what Faulkner said in *Intruder in the Dust*:

For every Southern boy fourteen years old, not once but whenever he wants it, there is the instant when it's still not yet two o'clock on that July afternoon in 1863 … and it's all in the balance, it hasn't happened yet, it hasn't even begun yet … and that moment doesn't need even a fourteen year old boy to think This time. Maybe this time with all this much to lose and all this much to gain.

"I love that passage, and I think of it today because it captures the pregnancy of that moment when Jason's shot is in the air. Please God let it go in. That is not blasphemy because it is just what jumps into my heart and of course I know God doesn't care whether it goes in or not.

"But in that moment, we had in our hearts and minds, proleptically I think the theologians would say, the joy of having it go in. Before it was not in, it was as good as in. For that fraction of a second, we had that experience, and it is enough. It is well worth the journey. At least for me it is, and I guess the ultimate point of this too-long post is that I hope it is also worth it for Jason. He took the shot. He gave us that moment. He trusted, and all we can do is be sure our reaction is worthy of that trust.

"Our responsibility, if that's not putting it too boldly, is to be alert to the value of that moment, to cherish it and remember it. (Henry V one more time: "This story shall the good man teach his son.") Stan's brilliant post elsewhere says well some important things about Davidson. All those things are distilled in the fraction of a second that shot is in the air. They are in the reactions of the players, the coaches, the families, the fans. I have been amazed how many people were watching and truly seemed to care about what happened.

"One wonders if we are too partisan, too fond of our own reputation, in our feelings about what happened in those four games. There is a danger of that, but if nothing else, the short attention span of the public (see the current issue of SI, which says almost nothing about the game) will keep us from going too far overboard.

"But I choose to see the end of the Kansas game as one of the most wonderful things I have ever seen, one of the best experiences I have ever had, and I thank everybody who helped make it possible. I don't know why the fates of basketball couldn't have smiled on us one more time to let that shot go in. But they didn't. This is the experience we have been given to digest, and I'm increasingly convinced that it is as it should be.

"Coach McKillop said it was about Trust. That goal was not missed."

—

It made people cry. I watched this in Detroit.

It made people preach. Literally. At least two Davidson-educated pastors delivered sermons in April about their alma mater's basketball team.

"I want to speak about that journey of recent weeks," the Rev. John M. Willingham said on April 13, 2008, at Doylestown Presbyterian Church in Doylestown, Pennsylvania, "because there was something about that experience for me which went beyond the hard court and became far more than a matter of who won or lost, as I began to see some things with different eyes."

Said the Rev. David J. Bailey on April 20, 2008, at Central Presbyterian Church in Anderson, South Carolina: "Weeping may tarry for the night, but joy comes with the morning."

"What was it? What was I watching?" Sonya Curry, June 11, 2008, Charlotte. Both these questions were hers. Her answer: "It was the platform that God gave that team. Look. This is what it is: love, joy, peace, patience, kindness, goodness, gentleness and self-control – the fruits of the spirit."

"What is winning?" Fan Sally Gordon, June 18, 2008, Davidson.

made one man Chris Gruber, June 16, 2008, Davidson. His son is Timothy Gruber. The conversation happened the week after the Final Four.

"We found something" Alum Sue McAvoy, May 1, 2008, by phone.

"We're all seeking it" Fan Tom Grogan, June 13, 2008, Davidson.

On the moment:

Fan Reed Jackson, May 6, 2008, Cornelius, North Carolina: "It was a weird feeling. I felt like it wasn't about wins and losses anymore. The fact that the moment existed made it worth experiencing."

Eileen Keeley, Davidson Vice President for College Relations, June 20, 2008, Davidson: "My feeling was: Oh my God. We're going to do this. Oh my God. We're going to go to the Final Four. Then: Wait. Don't get my hopes up too high. Don't jinx this by going overboard. It was almost a panicky feeling. Don't project beyond this moment. But the fact that we had the ball, and all this confidence in this team, I wasn't worried. This team was different. I just had such confidence they could do it. But wait. Stop. Focus on the moment. And then it felt so quick to me. I couldn't believe it was over."

Alum Stephen Cefalu, May 4, 2008, by phone: "Something I want to do better in life is live out those moments. Embrace them fully. Don't think about your savings account. Embrace the moment. I was wrestling with that during the moment: Don't think about San Antonio or how we're going to do that. Live life. Life should be about those moments, and they're so quick."

Alum Stan Brown, May 7, 2008, by phone: "There was not the sense of disappointment that I was expecting."

—

Tuesday evening in April I was there and later re-watched a tape provided by Davidson sports information director Marc Gignac.

—

Thursday evening in May I was there.